Jobs in the House and Garden

Jobs in the House and Garden

Based on the Yorkshire Television Series

MIKE SMITH and GORDON COOPER

in association with Robert Tattersall and Michael Beeston

STANLEY PAUL LONDON

STANLEY PAUL & CO LTD
3 Fitzroy Square, London W1

AN IMPRINT OF THE HUTCHINSON GROUP

London Melbourne Sydney Auckland
Wellington Johannesburg Cape Town
and agencies throughout the world

First published 1972

ISBN 0 09 111460 8 (cased)
0 09 111461 6 (paper)

This book has been set in Imprint type, printed by offset litho at Flarepath Printers Ltd., Watling St., Colney St., St. Albans, Herts and bound by William Brendon at Tiptree Essex.

Contents

Introduction

This book is as its title suggests—a variety of jobs that the average householder is either forced to tackle or that he can be encouraged to tackle. We don't cover everything—although you can learn here how to fix a tap, you'll have to buy a specialist book if you want to fit your own central heating system. Similarly, you can read how to disguise the hole left by that old fireplace you have just removed—but we don't dream to suggest you should take up plastering in order to do it! This was the idea behind our television series and this, we feel, is how most readers want it.

But jobs suggest maintenance and that is a horribly dull word. We don't look at it entirely like this. Some essential jobs are maintenance, are hard work and are dull—digging is one of them. Hints on digging, therefore must be included here (and we hope you will find them helpful and time saving). But there is another side to the coin—jobs are also improvements to the look and efficiency of your home, so we think you will like to know about house plants and how to set them out to advantage, we think you may like to know how to build a patio and a patio table.

And some of the jobs we cover are included because they are creative and provide some fun—simple renovations to a handsome but battered chest of drawers, growing plants from cuttings. This last example points our attitude exactly. No gardener can ignore the need for weed control, lawn maintenance etc.—however you look at such activities, there is no denying they are hard work. But gardens are for growing things, so we concentrate less upon stock maintenance, even though it takes up a vast proportion of time spent in the garden, than upon what to grow, where and how to grow it. This is a book for those who want to do all sorts of things in their garden and want to do them well, but who are not obsessed with perfection and dislike of failure.

A note about tools

This note is mainly with enjoyment in mind, but it can't be too often said—buy good quality tools, both for the home and garden. Furthermore, buy as many tools as you can afford—this is not extravagance. As we suggested above, our purpose is not to grind you into the ground with hard work. We hope you will actually enjoy some of your work. The right tool for the job gets that job done better and quicker and that means more enjoyably.

We all know of the usual tools—hammers, screwdrivers, spades and forks. Don't forget that new tools are continually being developed. Some of these were developed to be more versatile editions of established tools, some to do a particular job better.

Let the first job around your home or garden be to take a good look at your tools, replacing the old and worn, bringing them up to the decent minimum and then taking a look round for a few luxuries. Here are a few items which might interest you:

Garden tools in general. It is true that stainless steel tools cost a great deal and that mirror polished steel costs even more. Whether or not you think them worth the money only you can say. What we can say is that once you have used stainless steel, you'll never want to use anything else. Spades slice through soil in such a way that you can barely wait to lean into the next spadeful; halfway down a long bed you will bless yourself for buying it.

The "Skrake". A grass rake which takes up dead grass etc. as you pull and clears itself as you push.

The "automatic" spade. No good for trenching but for straight digging of soil it can cut down work and save bending. Operates on a spring principle and also has a fork fitment.

The "swoe". Cross between a "Dutch" push hoe and the draw hoe. You might like it but try to get it demonstrated. Not cheap.

The "surform". A cross between a file and a plane, and remarkably versatile.

"Posidrive" screwdriver and screws. With precision cross instead of a slot and blade; much more positive.

Push-pull screwdriver. With chuck and various bits—no twisting, just a pumping action; easy, safe and more controllable.

A "Mole" wrench. Gets a really firm grip; like a small hand vice.

A "Goscut". All-purpose shears for cutting any sheet material, such as hardboard, thin metal, laminates, etc.

Multi-purpose saw. For cutting asbestos or wood or thin metal.

Plane with replaceable blade. Change blades in your plane like blades in your razor; no sharpening required.

MIKE SMITH and GORDON COOPER

PART 1 JOBS IN THE HOUSE

1

Simple electricity

MIKE SMITH

Where better to start the book? Electricity lies at the core of every modern home, as we all learned to our cost during the power workers strike.

I am often asked how I feel about the do-it-yourselfer tackling electrical work. Well, I can put it in a nutshell. Any reasonably competent handyman has the skills needed to carry out small electrical jobs around the home. And yet, the consequences of even a minor error can be disastrous. Make a mistake when you are doing carpentry and all you have to do is scrap the piece of wood you have bodged up and start again. But if you slip up whilst you are tampering with electricity you can actually kill yourself.

Still, every householder is bound at some time to get involved in some kind of electrical work, even if it is merely a case of fitting a plug-end to some new item of equipment. And even here there is a right and wrong way to set about things.

If your electrical wiring is old fashioned, then the problems of fitting a plug end are greatest. For an old fashioned system of wiring will have probably three different sizes of socket outlet; each of them protected by a differently rated fuse back at the meter cupboard. There will be a 2 amp outlet, intended only for lighting, a 5 amp for small electrical appliances, and 15 amp for the bigger ones. The really heavy users of power, such as cookers and water heaters, are not to be regarded as portable appliances that can be plugged into socket outlets. They need to be independently wired to their own circuits.

Now it is important that you find out the rating of the appliance you have bought, so that you can fit the correct size of plug, and use it in the right outlet. The rating should be stamped on the machine somewhere, or given in the instruction booklet. If you are in doubt, ask at the shop where you bought it. If you fit a plug that allows you to connect your new appliance to a socket protected by a fuse of too low a rating, then the minute you switch on, the fuse will blow. So if you do not have an outlet of the correct size in a conveniently handy position, then I am afraid you will have to ask an electrician to come and install one for you.

You may think there is an easy way out, and that would be to go to the meter cupboard and stick a fuse of a higher rating into the wiring of the small socket. It would be the height of folly to do this, for the whole circuit is just not intended to stand up to the higher load. I do beg of you never to contemplate such a dangerous practice.

If your wiring is modern, then your problems are easier, for all the socket outlets will be connected to what is known as a ring main, and they will all be of the same size. There is also one other important difference about the ring main—although the whole circuit is protected by a fuse, each individual plug has its own fuse, too. This fuse will be of the cartridge type and not a length of wire, such as you will find in most meter cupboard fuse boxes. The rating of fuse in the plug should, of course, match the appliance to which it is fitted. At one time, there used to be four different sizes of fuse sold for a ring main plug—2, 5, 10 and 13 amp. This number has now been cut to two. Once again look to see what size of fuse your appliance needs, but as a general rule you can take it that if it has a rating of over 500 watt then a 13 amp fuse is required; otherwise fit a 3 amp fuse. The plug when you buy it will already have a fuse fitted, but it may be the wrong size. Tell the shopkeeper what size you want and he will change it for you. If you buy your plug at the same time as the appliance, then the dealer should automatically fit one of the correct size. Of course, the plug may not be a new one. You may have had it for some time, perhaps fitted to an appliance that you eventually discarded. Check the rating of the fuse in it before you fit it to something else, and change the fuse if needed—fuses are cheap enough to buy.

Earthed plugs

Most electrical items today need to be earthed, although some are sufficiently well insulated that earthing is not needed. Your instruction book should make it clear which type you have bought but a glance at the lead will tell you anyway. For an appliance that needs earthing will have three wires in the lead, whereas one that does not will have only two. Some of the socket outlets in an out of date wiring system may take only two pins and, even in a house with a ring main, there will be the lighting system, which will probably be a two-wire system. Never connect a three-wire appliance to a two-pin outlet—i.e. one without earth. You are putting yourself in danger if you do. It is downright foolish to get rid of the earth connection that has been put there specifically for your protection.

Of course, to make sure of this protection, it is vital that you connect up the right wire to the right terminal inside the plug. If it's a brand new item you are dealing with, then there is (or should be) no problem for the manufacturer ought to have affixed a sticker telling you which colour of wire goes to which point. But it's when you are wiring up an appliance not just fresh from the shop that the trouble arises. So here to refresh your memory is the correct colour coding—the brown wire should be connected to the live terminal, which is usually marked L, the blue wire to the negative terminal, marked N, and the green and yellow wire to the earth (E). Should it be a very old appliance, one that was sold before we went over to the new international coding system, then it will be red for live, black for negative, and green for earth.

If your appliance does not have an earth wire but only a live and a negative, then it is not so important to connect up to the correct point; but if the wires do have a colour coding, then it is just as easy to fit them correctly.

Fitting a plug end is an easy though fiddling sort of job, but there is one part of it that can be so irritating as to drive people almost to distraction. And that is baring the wires. You now how it goes. You use scissors or pen knife, and it seems impossible to take off the covering without cutting through some of the strands, too. You might have got to the stage where you have successfully bared two wires, then just as you think you are going to complete the third . . . snip. Through the wires you go. Because the three lengths are now all wrong, you have to start at the beginning again.

Well, there is one way to avoid all this irritation and that is to get a wire stripper. This is a most useful tool that quickly and efficiently strips off the insulation, without cutting the wire. It costs only about 30 pence. I think you will find it invaluable whenever you have to do electrical work.

Mending a fuse

Apart from fitting a plug, one other occasion when we all have to get involved in electricity is when a fuse blows. When this happens, first try to determine what has caused it. You will usually be only too well aware of where the trouble has originated, for the fuse will go when, say, you switch on the light in a back bedroom, or perhaps plug in a vacuum cleaner.

If it is a ring main to which the appliance has been plugged, then your problems are easier, for the fuse that will have blown should be the one in the plug end, and the ring main itself should be untouched and fully operational, although it is as well to check this point by connecting another appliance to the socket where the trouble originated. If this does not work either, test other sockets in your home in the same way. Should none of them work, then the trouble is in the ring itself, and you need the services of an electrician. But this will happen only in rare cases, and we can assume that it is simply a case of there being something wrong with your appliance. In fact, take off the plug top and you will probably be able to see if it is the fuse there that has blown. You will then know that the item must not be used again until it has been attended to.

But if the fuse goes when you switch on a room light or use a socket that is not connected to a ring, then switch off the light or unplug the appliance and go to your meter box. The first thing you must do when you open the door is switch off the electricity supply. In fact, switching off is something that you must do every time you are about to tamper with your wiring. I want to stress this point very strongly, because it is one that you can so easily forget. So get into the habit, of asking yourself before each step in the process: have I switched off?

Now it is difficult for me to say exactly what you will see inside every meter cupboard in the country but, as well as the dials that tell the meter reader how much electricity you have used, there will be a whole set of fuses, each one protecting some part of your wiring. A really prudent householder would have taken the trouble to find out long before any trouble cropped up, which fuse covered what. I know this is being wise after the event, but tracking down your wiring system is not a difficult task. This is what you do: switch on all the lights in your house, then go to the meter cupboard, switch off the main, remove one fuse, switch on again, and notice which lights do not come on. Carry on in this way until you have traced the fuses covering all the lights—you will notice that there will be two or three, perhaps even more, lighting circuits in your home, each of them having its fuse.

Now you have to try to track down the power system, and it's just the same process. Switch off, remove a fuse, switch on, then plug in to each of your sockets, noting which will not supply power. Having satisfied yourself as to what job every fuse in the box is doing, there is one final measure you can take to show how really prudent you are. And that is to go off to your electrical shop, and buy a stock of fuse wire, to be kept next to the fuses so that it will always be to hand. At the same time, incidentally, get a torch, which should also have a permanent home inside the meter cupboard, so that you will be able to see what you are doing if a fault develops in the lighting circuit after dark.

But let us get back to the blown fuse. There are two basic kinds of fuse. The most modern is of the cartridge variety—it will, in short, be a bigger version of the fuse you fit into a ring main plug. But most homes in Britain have what are known as rewireable fuses—in other words, they use fuse wire.

When a cartridge fuse blows, you merely take out the damaged one and replace it with a new one of the correct rating. The rating will usually be given on the holder, but basically you use a 5 amp fuse for the lighting circuit, 15 amp for power, and 30 amp for a cooker or water heater.

If you have a rewireable fuse, take out the porcelain holder, remove the remains of the old wire, and clean everything up. Cut a length of new wire of the currect rating. Once again, the rating should be given somewhere but the amperages given above basically apply, except that if you do not have a ring main some of the power outlets may be less than 15 amp. Wrap one end of the wire round one of the retaining screws, and drive the screw home. Feed the wire along to the screw at the other end and repeat the process. The wire must be looped round the screws clockwise or it will come undone as the screw is turned.

Now you can switch on the main and everything should be all right. But the one thing you must not do is plug in the appliance or switch on the light that caused the trouble in the first place, otherwise you will have a blown fuse all over again, the only difference being that this time you will know exactly which one is causing all the trouble.

No, basically, you need an electrician or appliance repairer to find out what went wrong. There is just one check you can make for yourself. One very common cause of a fuse blowing is the live wire coming loose and touching the negative one, or vice versa. So switch off at the main, remove the cover plate of the room light switch and see if everying is connected up properly there. If it is, make a similar check to the ceiling rose, and the light socket.

Should a portable appliance in a socket be the trouble then, once again making sure you have switched off, remove the cover plate of the outlet and check the connections. Check, too, the connections of the plug, and the other end of the lead should it be an item such as an electric sweeper that has a loose one.

If you do not come across the cause of the trouble this way, then I would advise to proceed no further, unless you really do know quite a bit about electricity. I think you ought to call in professional help.

2

Simple plumbing

MIKE SMITH

Along with electricity, there is one other trade that do-it-yourselfers often wonder whether they ought to tackle, and that is plumbing. Now the consequences of failure in plumbing are not so severe as with electricity—you cannot kill or maim yourself if you do not connect up your pipework properly. But you can put yourself to a lot of inconvenience and cause a lot of damage, if you get water flooding all over the place. And this is the prospect that alarms a lot of would-be amateur plumbers.

Well, all I can say is that plumbing work is carried out regularly by keen amateurs in every part of the country. One form this commonly takes is the installation of a full central heating system. A lot of heating firms in Britain now specialize in supplying central heating in kit form, along with a full instruction book, so that householders can put in their own central heating system. And these firms will tell you amazing stories of how people with no experience whatsoever—a lot of them women, some of them elderly—successfully tackle the installation of a complete hot water and central heating system. Now I am not suggesting that you take on anything so ambitious as *your* first job. But there are a lot of minor plumbing tasks that are most certainly within your competence. Let us take a look at what is involved.

Before you think of doing any plumbing, however, I would ask you first to examine the water pipes in your home, especially if you live in an old house. A long time ago lead was used for these pipes, then later on galvanized steel. If your pipework is made of either of these metals, then I have to advise you not to try to

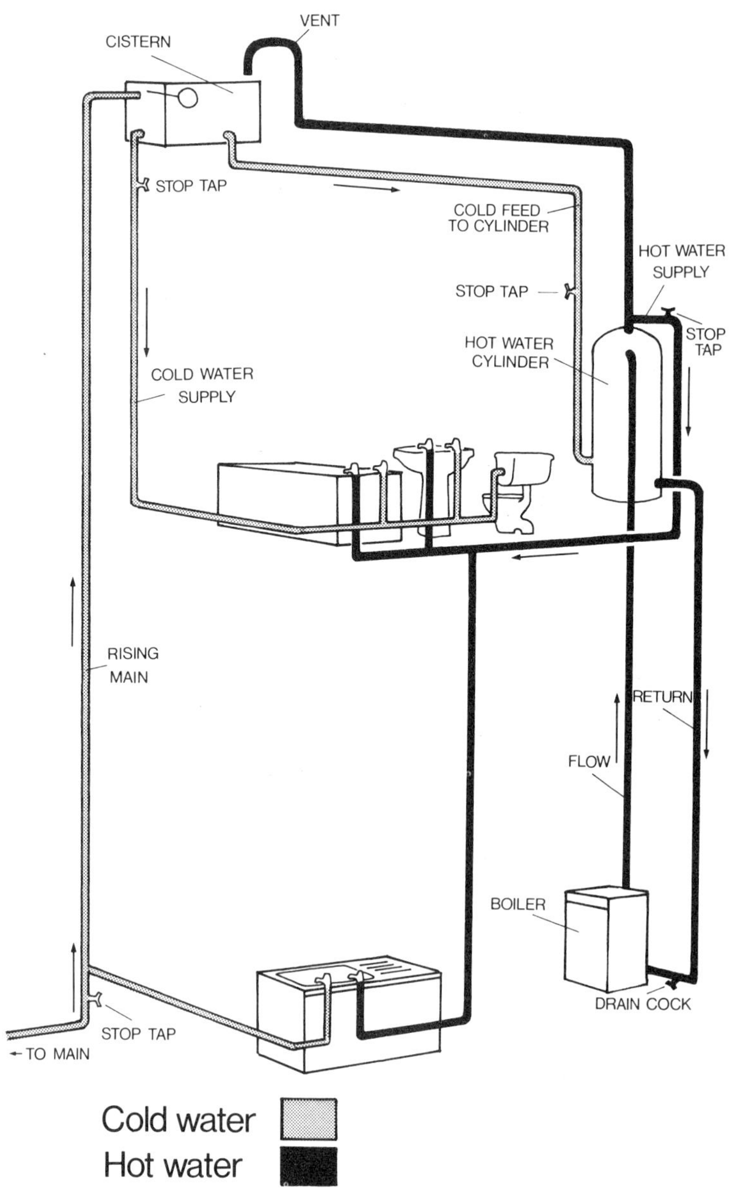

A typical domestic water system.

interfere with it. For handling these pipes requires a lot of specialised skill and knowledge. But in between the wars, copper pipework started to be used and if your house was built since then, or, in the case of an older house, if the plumbing system has been brought up to date recently, then it should be copper pipes that have been used. With these plumbing is a much simpler operation. You will be able to recognise copper immediately by its colour.

How the plumbing system works

There are bound to be differences in many parts of the country but this is it, by and large. Water comes to you from the board's main, and there are usually two stop cocks—one where the pipe enters your land, and the other where it enters the house. This pipe is known as the rising main. Soon after the rising main stop cock, there will be a Tee-off to the kitchen tap so that, for drinking and cooking, you are using pure mains water. The pipe will then carry water up to the cold storage tank and it is this tank that feeds the cold taps through the rest of the house (in some areas, all cold taps are taken direct from the main, but many water boards frown on this) and the hot water cylinder. The fact that water emerging from your cold taps (apart from your kitchen tap) will have come from a tank in the loft where it will have collected dust, and dead insects, perhaps even have been fouled by birds, is one reason why you should never use it for drinking or cooking. The water in the hot cylinder is heated by some means or other and pipes lead from it to all the hot outlets throughout the house. That is the theory. It is a good idea to look at your plumbing system to see how it works out on the ground. Apart from anything else, you will then have a good idea of what is happening, should there ever be an emergency.

The lengths of pipe that make up the system are connected up by what are known as joints—do not get confused with those things the carpenter cuts in wood. There are two basic types of copper joint. The one the tradesman usually uses, because it is cheaper, is the capillary joint. This joint incorporates a ring of solder at the end. You clean up the connection thoroughly with steel wool, coat it with flux, and push the ends of the pipes to be connected into the joint. Then you play a blowlamp flame on each end to melt the solder. The knack comes in knowing exactly how long to heat the joint. Too little and the solder will not melt

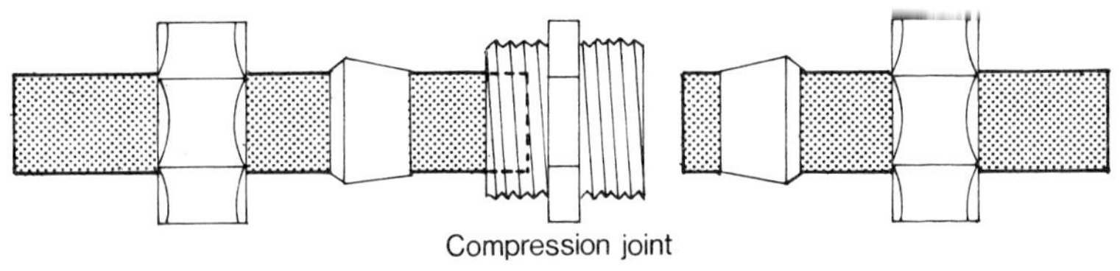

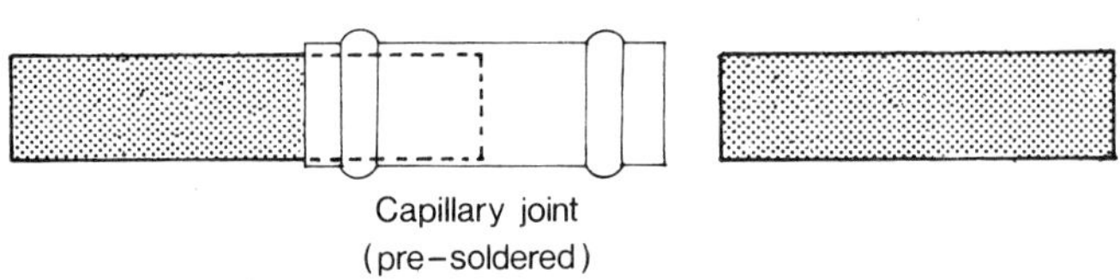

The two methods of joining copper tube in plumbing.

properly and flow all round the pipe to form an effective seal; too much and the solder will run out too far, again resulting in a leaky joint. What you should do is apply heat until a bright silver ring appears indicating that the solder has flooded the joint. Then withdraw the heat immediately. Really, it is quite easy but it takes practice to get the timing just right. Because of that, many amateurs prefer to use the compression joint.

This consists of three parts—the union, which is really the body of the joint; the coupling nut, which screws on to the threaded portion of the union; and a soft copper collar, known as an olive. You push first the coupling nut then the olive on to the end of the pipe you wish to join. Push the end of the pipe into the union, then tighten up the nut. As the nut is tightened, it crushes the olive and presses it lightly around the pipe. Thus a waterproof seal is formed. You can, if you wish to make doubly sure, smear a bit of BossWhite on to the joint, but it is not strictly necessary.

A compression joint as you can see is very easy to handle. There is just one mistake that most amateurs make when using it. They tend to overtighten the nut. If you do this, the olive can be squashed flat down to the diameter of the pipe itself, without touching the inside of the union. Thus, it will not form a seal. The correct method is to turn the nut with your fingers as tight as it will go. Then give one full turn with a spanner. This should be quite enough to make the joint water tight, but when the water is eventually switched on examine your work, and, if the joint is weeping, turn the nut slightly once again, using a spanner.

The compression joint costs more than the capillary one, which is why professionals do not make such extensive use of it. But you will be using so few of them that this point is not likely to bother you.

The examples of these joints that I have shown in the sketches are just straight connectors, but, in fact, a wide variety is available. For instance, you can get T-joints, angled joints, and joints with different sized threads for connecting up the three sizes of pipe commonly used in domestic plumbing—$\frac{1}{2}$, $\frac{3}{4}$ and 1 inch.

But you not only have to carry water to a tap or appliance; you have to get rid of the waste. Once again, modern materials have made things easier for the amateur, for plastic waste pipes are now available. These are easily cut with an all-purpose saw or hacksaw, and easily joined. Various joints are sold, and in some cases you merely click the various parts together for a push fit, whilst in others you may have to use a jointing compound—do exactly what the makers say.

Fitting a stop tap

So, what can you do with this little knowledge I have given you? Well, one thing you could do to gain confidence is fit a few stop taps here and there. I feel that the average domestic plumbing system is not sufficiently well protected by stop taps. You should be able to shut off whole sections of your water system quickly should there be a burst, or you want to carry out modifications. Two points where there ought to be stop taps are at the outlet from the cold storage tank, and the outlets from the hot water cylinder. Turn off the water at the main and turn on all relevant taps until the flow stops. For instance, if it were the cold tank outlet you were dealing with, you would open all the cold taps connected to it—which would usually mean those in the bathroom—until it was empty. Buy a stop tap that matches the size of pipe and that is fitted by means of compression joints. If you look at the side of it, you will probably spot an arrow. This shows you the direction of water flow. Make sure you fit it the right way round. Use a hacksaw to cut out enough length of pipe to take the tap, and fit it just as though it were any ordinary compression joint.

Plumbing in a washing machine

Do you feel a little more ambitious now? Well, what about plumbing-in a washing machine, or dishwasher? You must read what I am about to say now in conjunction with the maker's instructions, for he may have stipulations to make about the height of the drain outlet from the floor etc. Look for a suitable position on a cold pipe, and fit there a branch pipe, by means of a T compression joint. Run a length of copper pipe to a point convenient for connecting up with your appliance, by means of its flexible hose. A worm-drive clip will probably be recommended for this. Somewhere in the pipe though, and at a point convenient for you, you must fit a stop tap, for you never know when the machine will have to be disconnected for servicing, or indeed be dispensed with entirely. If you did not have this stop tap, you would have to turn off your domestic supply when you wanted to remove the machine. Finally, if the pipe is in any great length, it should be supported to the wall with clips.

It is as well, incidentally, always to turn off a washing machine's or dishwasher's stop tap when you go to bed, since during the night, when not much water is being used, you can get a big enough build-up of pressure in the main to blow off the connection of the flexible hose to the copper piping. It is a very rare happening, this, I know, but so little effort is involved in turning off that you may think it worth it.

Now what about the waste water from the machine? You can, of course, just let the appliance's drain hose trail into the sink, because after all it is a plumbed-in water supply that is the main thing, since it gets rid of all the inconvenience of fitting the intake hose on to your taps. But you can, if you wish, go the whole hog and have proper waste disposal.

This can present difficulties in very modern installations, where there is a one-pipe system of drainage. I don't want to be too technical, but just look outside your kitchen and see if the sink discharges into an open gulley. If it does, then you can go ahead.

Your waste system from the washing machine will be in 1½ or 1¼ inch plastic piping. Starting at the machine end of the system, you have the flexible plastic hose which should be fitted to a length of pipe, following the maker's instructions. To the other end of this pipe you fit a U-trap (again in plastic) which will stop drain smells from coming back into your kitchen. The pipework then

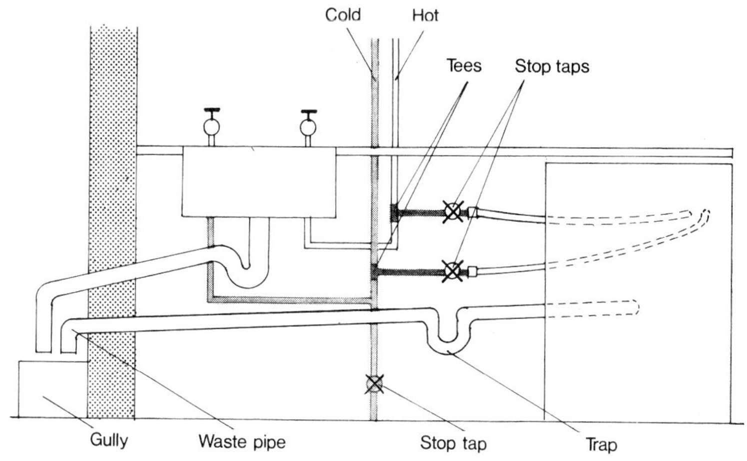

How a washing machine should be plumbed-in.

passes through the wall (knock out a hole with a hammer and cold chisel, then make good afterwards). It should finish below the grating but above the water level of the gutter. The whole system will be supported on clips fixed to the wall etc., as needed.

Your own particular circumstances will determine the path of the pipework. Work out the most convenient route from the appliance or the gulley, then study carefully a manufacturer's catalogue, plotting exactly which items from his range you need.

There is one other use for a compression joint, and that is making a repair in pipework, either after a burst, or when you accidentally damage it (see the chapter on floorboards). A compression joint is to be preferred here to a capillary one, for the latter needs perfectly dry pipework to function effectively.

After all this, I am sure you will begin to feel that plumbing need hold few terrors for you. I would hate to suggest that you become too ambitious but . . . *have* you got central heating in your home? It is estimated that you can cut the cost of installing central heating by as much as fifty per cent, if you do all the work yourself. Where is the rest of the money to come from? There are various loan schemes, and often your building society or bank will help. Why not write to one of the specialist firms dealing in DIY central heating. You will find them very helpful.

3

Insulating your house

MIKE SMITH

We all rate a warm home as one of the most important of creature comforts and each year at the end of summer you will find people scanning the brochures put out by heating firms. They will be looking what new electric fires are available, wondering whether to put a gas fire in place of that old open fire in the living room or else replace it with an up-to-date solid-fuel stove, perhaps debating whether this year at last they can afford central heating.

And yet I can't help thinking that perhaps they are starting the wrong way around. For, instead of dreaming up better ways of pumping more heat into their homes, they should perhaps be making sure that whatever heat is already in there doesn't get out. In other words, they ought to be making insulation their first priority. I know dozens of cases where people have improved the insulation of their home and have found as a result that they do not need a bigger fire in the living room, that the small fan heater they use for the bedroom is quite adequate and that, after all, their central heating system is not underpowered. Now I don't say this will be so in every case but it is worth trying out. Anyway, even if improving your home's insulation doesn't make it unnecessary to buy extra appliances, it will succeed in cutting your fuel bills in future.

So let's take a look at how heat escapes from your home. It will get out through the roof, through badly fitting doors and windows, through the glass of the windows itself, even via the walls. But, since heat tends to rise, the most important escape route is going to be via the roof. In fact, the experts have estimated that twenty per cent of the heat loss of an uninsulated house will be via the roof. So obviously it pays you to start your insulation drive here.

Insulating the roof

In a normal house, where there is space in the roof, then the way to do this is to lay insulating material on the floor of the loft. There are two types of insulating material. One is a blanket that you roll between the joists—you buy it in standard widths to fit the gap. The other is a loose-fill material that you pour in place. The blanket, which can be of either glass fibre or mineral wool, is the most popular, and it can be bought in three thicknesses—1 inch, 2 inches or 3 inches. Obviously, the thicker the material the more you will be charged for it but my advice is to buy the thickest you can afford.

If you are using a loose-fill material, which will be small pellets of either vermiculite or mineral wool, then obviously you decide for yourself how thick a layer you are going to put down. I would recommend that this should be at least 2 inches, and more if you can afford it.

Now it is no use pretending that doing any sort of job in your loft is a pleasant way of passing the time . . . it isn't. You will be working in a dark, dirty, insect-ridden place. Unless you are very lucky and have a loft with a high roof space, you will have to be crouching or lying down the whole time. But should you ever think of faltering, then I suggest you let your mind dwell on all those heating costs you will be saving, and let that be your inspiration. But now let's get down to some more practical advice.

The "floor" of a loft consists of a series of joists to the underside of which will be fixed the ceiling of the room below. This ceiling is simply not strong enough to take your weight if you stand on it, so you must be careful to avoid doing so or you will cause damage that it will cost you a lot of money to have put right—repairs to a plaster ceiling are not easy for an unskilled amateur to carry out. You might feel that you are perfectly capable of balancing on the joists, but many a man has learned to his cost that it isn't so easy. You will be spending a fair amount of time in that loft, you will have to reach and stretch, and, before you know where you are, you will have put your foot in it. No, the only thing to do is take a stout plank (test first that it is strong enough to support your

Unrolling blanket between the joists.

weight) up into the loft, and lay it across the joists. Then stand on this whilst you work. Obviously, the longer the plank is the better, for you will then not have to move it around so often. But a combination of the height of the roof space, the size of the trap-door opening, and the amount of room for manoeuvre on the landing down below, will impose restrictions. If you do have to cut the plank to size, try to ensure that it spans exactly across an exact number of joists. For if there is an overhang, there is just a chance that you might step on it. The resulting see-saw effect could send you crashing through the ceiling, and the other end of the plank up through the tiles on the roof.

Once you are up in the loft and standing on your plank, you will need to see what you are doing, so one of your first priorities will be to drive a nail into some convenient structural member and hang a light from it. A torch would be better than nothing, but the sort of inspection lamp that mechanics use on a car is ideal. There is no need to buy one of these for they are easy to improvise, at least for this sort of job. All you need is a length of lighting flex with a plug at one end to fit into an electrical point down below, and the normal bayonet light fitting at the other. Loop a knot into the flex near the bayonet fitting, and it will then hang from a nail. Incidentally, such an arrangement is safe for use only in situations such as this. Don't be tempted to rig up something like it for use out of doors or in a garage.

Beware, too, of your hands. Some of the insulating materials, especially those with a glass content, can scratch them, so be sure to wear a pair of old gloves. Oh, and one final point . . . mind your head.

If it's blanket you are using, take the first roll up into the loft, place it in a far corner, and start to unroll between the joists. When you reach the end, cut the roll to length. Now lay the next length in the adjacent gap, and so on.

Loose-fill material is merely poured from a bag into the space between the joists. The point to watch here is to make sure you put down sufficient to create a thick enough layer—one of 1, 2 or 3 inches, according to whatever you have decided. You can do this by eye, but it is so easy to make a simple gauge that also acts as a spreader, and will do the job quickly and accurately for you. Take a piece of scrap wood and saw it to a length slightly greater than the distance between your joists. Now at each end of the wood make a couple of saw cuts to form two shoulders, so that you have created a sort of stubby-looking "T". This "T" sits on the joists and descends into the space between them. Its size should be such that beneath it there is a space equal to whatever thickness you want the layer of loose-fill to be. This little tool makes laying the stuff so easy. You just empty pellets into the voids, place the tool on the joists and move it along. It will thus spread the pellets to the required depth. Sometimes, of course, you will notice a space beneath the "T" and that will tell you you have to pour out more loose-fill.

Insulating the water tank and pipework

Most homes have a cold water tank, with associated pipework, up in the loft, and there's a risk here. For after you have insulated

Spreading loose-fill is easier if you make this 'T'.

your loft, it will be a much colder place, and there is thus a risk of a freeze-up in winter. The way to avoid this is to fit one of the special insulating kits to your tank.

Now for the pipework, which also needs protection. If the pipes are just about at joist level, or not much higher and you are using blanket, then there is a simple way out. You merely drape the blanket over the pipes, placing none underneath so that warm air can reach them as it rises from the rest of the house. This will tend to make them invisible, though, so you will have to take great care that you do not place your plank on top of them with the consequent risk of causing damage.

Should you be using the loose fill method, or for pipes placed on high, lagging will have to be used. There are quite a few methods you can use to lag pipes. Offcuts of blanket can be tied to them, felt can be wrapped round them, and so on. But I like the purpose-made tubes that you clip on. They are quicker and

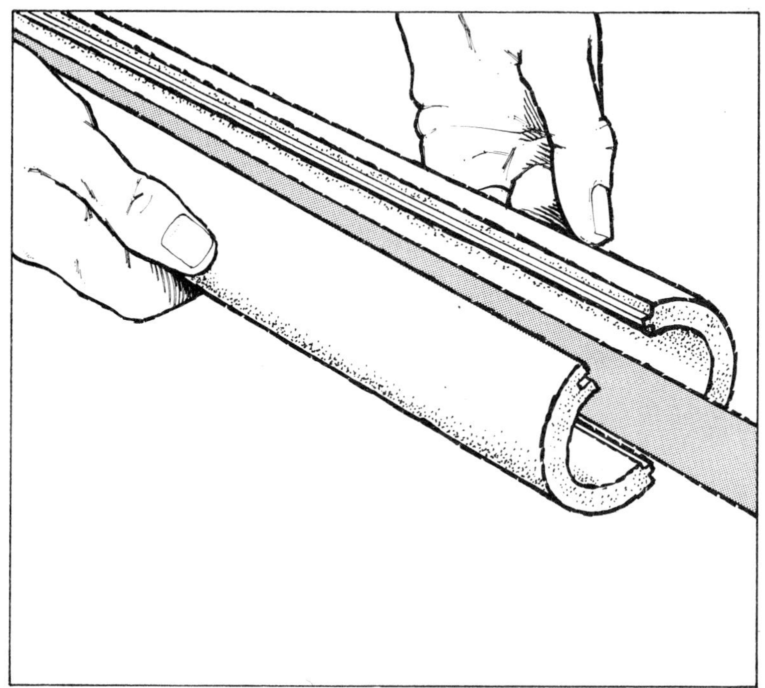

Lagging to protect pipes against frost.

easier to fix, and you can be sure you will have done a good job.

And while you are in the loft . . .

As you have gone to all the trouble of getting up into your loft and rigging up a light etc., I think it is just as well to take a look around. Search particularly for any signs of woodworm attack, and deal with it. If the attack is local, you can probably cope with it yourself by treating the affected area with woodworm killer. If it looks more serious it is better to call in one of the specialist firms. Some of these will give you a free survey, without any obligation whatsoever, and tell you what treatment is needed.

Look, too, for any signs of damage up there. Should there be any gaps between the slates or tiles, you will see them much more clearly from up inside your loft, than you would by carrying out an inspection whilst you stand in your back garden. If your house is terraced or semi-detached, look to see if there are any bricks

Sticking tiles to a ceiling.

missing in the party walls with the house or houses next door. If you do spot any gaps, fill them up, for this is an important route for noise to pass to your house from next door. And if anything at all looks wrong with any structural timbers, call in an expert to look at them.

Insulating with ceiling tiles

Of course, some houses do not have any roof space and so you simply cannot go up into the loft to insulate it. What can you do then? I still think it is worth while carrying out some form of insulation, and perhaps the easiest method is to stick expanded polystyrene tiles to the ceiling. These came in for a great deal of criticism some time ago as being a fire risk. However, the Fire Research Station has now ruled that they are safe provided you do not fix them with the dab method (that is just using spots of adhesive) but coat the whole back of the tile.

You may have read that these tiles can be painted if they get dirty or tatty-looking. Well, so they can, but the Fire Research Station did find that this can be dangerous if you use a gloss paint. It recommends that you choose either a flame retardant paint (there are one or two on the retail market) or a matt finish emulsion.

This advice has given a new lease of life to these tiles, and several decorative ones can now be bought. As well as insulating your home, these can be quite a decorative feature, and they are an easy way of covering up a ceiling that is in bad condition.

Draughts and draught excluding

I suppose the second greatest source of heat loss in any home comes from cracks around doors and windows. In fact, so obvious a nuisance is this, with draughts whistling through to make everybody feel uncomfortable, that many people feel more heat escapes through those cracks than up through the roof. That is not so (at least it isn't so unless you have giant sized cracks) but it is worth trying to cut down on draughts.

In many homes, it will be uncomfortably obvious where the draughts originate—any icy blast will make itself known all the time. But often you can be aware of a vague feeling of being exposed to draughts without being entirely clear what is causing them. In these cases, light a candle or a taper and move it around likely sources of draught—near doors and windows, along skirting boards, near gaps in floor boards. Where the candle flickers, you will know there are draughts.

If your house is heated by an old fashioned open fire then the best and quickest thing you can do to free your home from draughts is to throw out the old grate as quickly as possible. For it is a prime cause of draughts. Any form of combustion uses air, but these museum pieces absolutely suck air in. What you replace it with doesn't matter—electric or gas fire, or modern solid fuel appliance—you will cut down dramatically on draughts. Even so—even in a room with no source of heat such as a bedroom—you might still get a certain amount of draughts, and there is no point in putting up with these.

The first thing is to fit draught excluders to exterior doors and opening windows. There are two main types of excluder—self-adhesive foam strip, and sprung metal. The foam strip is cheaper

How to enlarge a door that doesn't fit its frame properly.

to buy and quicker to fix in place. It can, however, come unstuck after prolonged exposure to wet weather, and it will perish after a time, thus losing its resilience. Sprung metal, or indeed resilient plastic strip, which you tack to the frame of a door or wooden window, is dearer but tends to last longer. Of course, you cannot nail anything to the frames of metal windows but that doesn't mean you can use only adhesive foam on them. Clip-on metal and plastic is available.

For a window, the draught excluder is fitted all round the opening. You cannot put the strip on the bottom of a door opening, however, for you would damage it as you walked across it. Instead, you must fit a special threshold strip. These usually have a strip, screwed to the step, that incorporates a flexible cushion that butts up against the bottom of the door. Often, too, there is a plate fixed to the bottom of the door to deflect wind-blown rain. These thresholds also have a secondary advantage that they make it more difficult for insects and vermin to crawl under the bottom of your door.

In many cases the draught-admitting gap is too big to be cured by any form of strip. Here is what you must do in those cases. First take the door or window off its hinges—you will need help with this, due to the weight of the door and the possibility of dropping the window and breaking the glass. Now take a length of wood whose width is slightly greater than the gap between door and frame. Glue and nail this to the opening edge of the door, and punch the nails well home. Now plane the edges of the strip of wood so that it lies flush with the door, and the face of it sufficiently for it to allow the door to close. What . . . you think you are not a sufficiently good carpenter to handle a plane? But planing is easy, and I explained exactly how to do it in the book I published in conjunction with my previous television series (Toolbox, 50p from Stanley Paul Ltd.). Now fix the door or window back on its hinges and you should have cured the draught problem.

But you get draught gaps not only between the frame and an ill-fitting door, but also between the frame and the wall to which it is fixed, as a result of the mortar seal cracking over the years. You can hack out the old mortar and re-point the gap if you wish, but special sealants are sold precisely for this job, and they are much easier for the handyman to handle. Your local do-it-yourself shop should stock them. So that you don't have to spend so much money on them, pack the gap with rope or old rags to within ½ inch of the surface, then just top off with sealant.

Another entry point for draughts in many homes is the floor. Over the years the floor boards shrink, and gaps appear between them. This gap will be all the more pronounced if boards with a square edge, instead of tongued and grooved, have been used. A similar sort of gap can appear, too, where the skirting board meets the floor.

Now many householders faced with the problem of draughts coming up through their floor take a long close look at their property, and think they have come up with the solution. For they see the airbrick let into their walls, and think all they have to do is block it up, and their problems will be solved.

But the course of action they propose is not only wrong; it is also downright dangerous. For those "holes" that they see are in fact an airbrick put there expressly for ventilation. Block up that airbrick, and the area under your floor will become a damp, dank place where the growth of all kinds of fungus and rot will be encouraged.

Sealing a crack round the window frame.

No, you must leave the airbrick severely alone. Well, perhaps that is not quite true. I have known instances where vermin, such as field mice, have found the airbrick a convenient point of entry into a house where they want to shelter for the winter. If you feel this is happening in your home, then you can cover the brick with wire netting, or perhaps better still plastic mesh, with holes too small to admit a mouse. But that is the only thing I would ever recommend anyone doing to an air brick.

So what can you do about draughts coming up through the floor? There are all kinds of material you can use for filling up the crack—thin strips of wood, rope and old newspaper covered up by stopping etc. But, really, the best thing of all is to lay some form of wall-to-wall floor covering (see Chapter 5). You can choose whatever you like, or can afford, to cover the floor—carpet and parquet are the most luxurious, but cheaper things such as vinyl, hardboard, flooring grade chipboard will all perform equally well the job of cutting out draughts.

If you choose a thin material such as vinyl, then that will not cover up the gap between skirting board and floor. In fact, in extreme cases, neither would some of the thicker materials. To cover this gap you must use moulding, which you pin to the skirting board, not the floor, Either triangular or quarter round section moulding will do. There is no need, incidentally, to use glue as well as pins.

Double glazing—should you or shouldn't you?

Once you have dealt with the roof and shut out the draughts, you will have eliminated the more serious heat losses in your home. There is another way, however, in which heat can get out of your home and that is through the glass of the windows. This is because the glass used in most domestic windows has poor insulating qualities, and just cannot keep the heat in. But there is another way in which windows make a room cooler; they actually cause draughts. For you must not imagine that draughts occur only when there is a gap to the outside air. They can actually be set up within the room itself. Now, remember, warm air rises, and, consequently, cold air falls. Now on a cold winter night the panes of your windows are going to become very cold. And they will cool the air near them inside the room. This air will thus be pushed

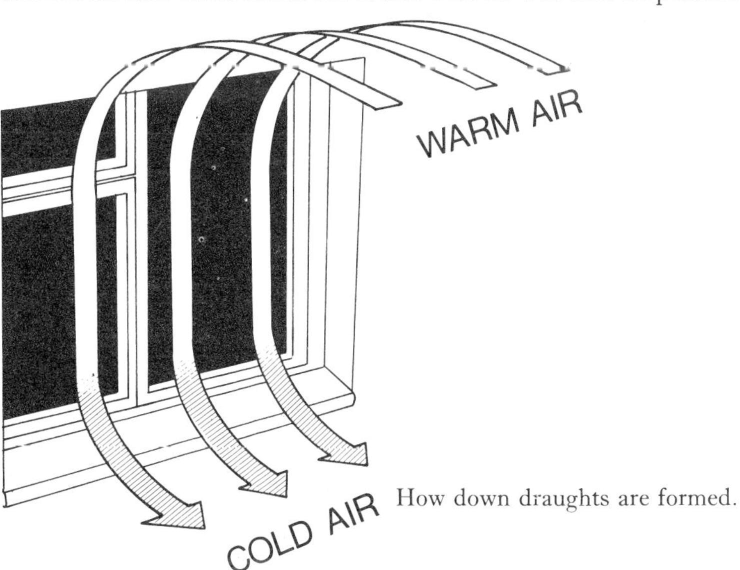

How down draughts are formed.

downwards, and a whole movement of air will have been set up. Heating engineers call this movement of air a downdraught, and it can be just as chilling and unpleasant as the real thing. In fact, if you think you have draughts in your home, but cannot for the life of you see where they are coming from, then it may well be that they are downdraughts. You should always bear the possibility of these in mind when you go a draught-hunting.

One cure for such draughts is double glazing. But wait before you rush out to buy some. A lot of points need to be taken into consideration.

First let us see how double glazing works. It consists of two, instead of the normal one, pane of glass, and between them is trapped a layer of air. It is this air, rather than the glass, that forms an effective insulating barrier. The air stops warm air from escaping out of the room, thus cutting down on heat loss. And it stops the inner pane of glass from being cooled, thus removing a cause of downdraught.

And doesn't it, you may also ask, cut down on noise transmission, so that you will be less troubled by the sounds of children at play, passing traffic and that ton-up kid across the way revving up his motor bike engine? Well, yes and no. For the critical thing about double glazing is the space between the two panes. The ideal distance for heat insulation is $\frac{3}{4}$ inch. Much less than this and the layer of air is not a thick enough cushion. Much more and there is enough room for downdraughts to be set up within the cavity, which will cool the inner pane and set up downdraughts inside the room. But for double glazing to be an effective sound barrier, the gap should be at least 4 inches. Any less and the blanket of trapped air would be too thin to cut off noise. So if you want to cut out sound and heat loss through windows at one and the same time, you really need triple glazing, with first two panes $\frac{3}{4}$ inch apart, then one spaced at least another 4 inch away. All of which would be going a bit too far for most people.

If already you are beginning to suspect that I am not an avid enthusiast for double glazing, then I have to admit that I have my reservations. A lot depends on what your house is like and the kind of life you lead, and I see it this way. It is true that double glazing will make a room warmer. But good quality curtains, especially if you line them with insulating material, will perform just as well as all but the most expensive double glazing systems.

Now it so happens that the coldest time of the year is also the one with least daylight, so that for the larger part of the time you would have the curtains drawn anyway. Furthermore, in most homes the window area is relatively small and the heat loss thus not all that great. Certainly, any money spent on double glazing would not give you the sort of bonus you can expect from insulating the loft. Another point, a window usually forms but a small proportion of a wall area and you are wasting your time insulating the glass if the wall is leaking out heat like mad.

Summing up, I would say that in a home with smallish windows where all the members of the family spend the daylight hours of the week out at work or at school, with Mum and Dad shopping on Saturdays and the youngsters playing sport, so that the only time they actually sit down in the living room during daylight is for an hour or so on Sunday afternoon, then probably double glazing would not be worth while. But in an ultra modern house with huge picture windows, where mother and the children are at home all day and the family together in the house at weekends, then double glazing is a necessity. Those are, of course, two extremes and most people would have a home and life style somewhere in between. Quite which side of the dividing line that makes double glazing worthwhile or otherwise *your* home comes is something you must decide in your own particular case.

Types of double glazing

There are three basic kinds of double glazing. The most effective and, equally, the most expensive are the factory sealed units. When you look at these, you would be hard put to it to spot the difference between them and the single pane of glass, but they are in fact two panes with air space in between them. There are two types of sealed unit. One has two panes of glass held together by a metal, alloy, or plastic edge. The other consists solely of glass, with the two panes fused together. Both kinds are sealed so that condensation cannot take place in the middle and you clean only two glass surfaces.

The first type of sealed unit is usually purpose-made and the second available in a range of standard sizes. Often though you have to alter your existing frames to receive them. By and large their installation is a job for the specialist, although there are some

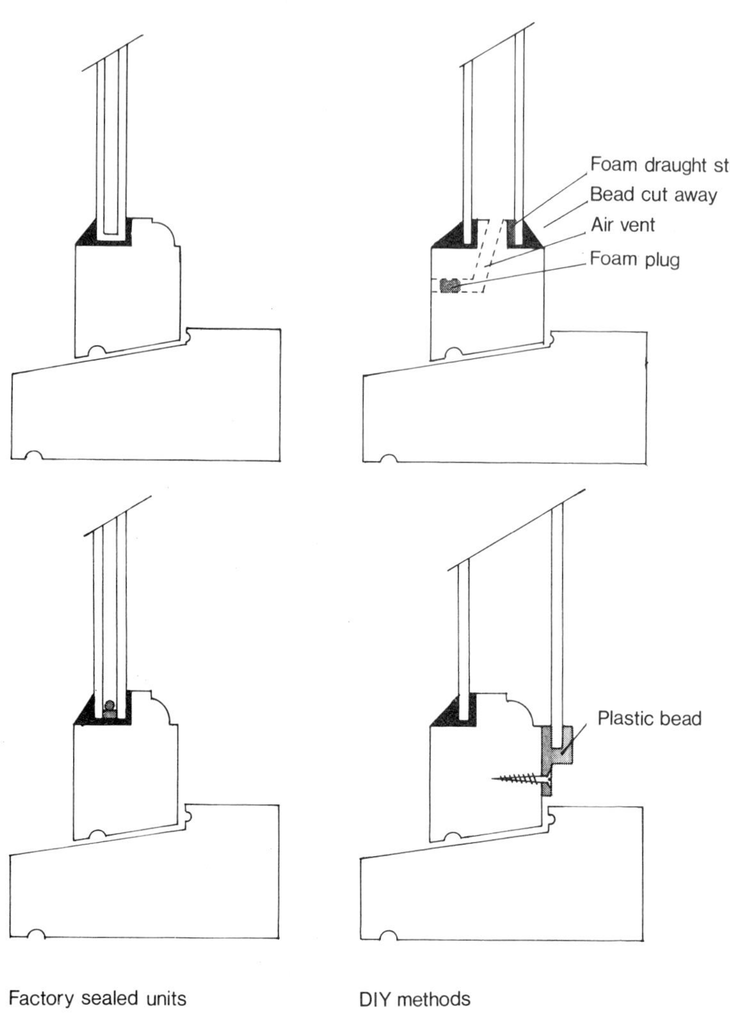

Types of double-glazing.

that the handyman can install himself, provided his frames are suitable.

The second type is known as the coupled sash. This consists of one single glazed window with an auxiliary one coupled to it, so that both can move together in the case of opening windows. The auxiliary window is usually fitted with some sort of hinge or

A double-glazing kit—the Grippa Frame.

fastener so that it can be moved when you want to clean the windows, for I am afraid there are four sides that need cleaning with this system. Generally, the coupled sash is installed in new buildings, although it is sometimes possible to modify existing windows so that they can accommodate them.

Finally, there is the secondary window, which normally comes as a lightweight aluminium or rigid plastic frame which is used to apply a second pane of glass to existing window frames. The secondary frame can come ready-made to measure for fixing. But the great interest of handymen in this type of double glazing is that he can buy it as a do-it-yourself kit in an inexpensive form. In this latter case, it will come in lengths of framing that he has to cut to size and the various kits adopt different means of joining the strips at the corner and fixing them to the frame. Once again there has to be some means of separating the secondary window from the main frame so that the four sides of glass can be cleaned.

You could, of course, devise your own system of secondary

window made up from rebated timber beading, but the kits can be so cheap that it probably is not worth your while to do so.

One of the snags of this type of double glazing is that the gap between the two panes is not hermetically sealed, and you can as a result get condensation there. One way to avoid this is to drill ¾ inch holes in the bottom of the main frame to permit ventilation. Windows more than 5 feet square will need two or more of these holes, and they should be plugged up with glass fibre or mineral wool insulation material to keep out dust and insects.

The order in which I have described these systems to you is in descending order of effectiveness but there is no doubt that the cheaper ones do have some effect. With the reservations I outlined initially, their installation can be beneficial.

With compliments

Yorkshire Television Limited
The Television Centre
Leeds LS3 1JS
0532 38283 Telex 557232

4

Floors and floorboards

MIKE SMITH

In between the ceiling of one room and the carpet of the room above lies what to many people is a forbidding area—the floor and floor cavity. If something goes wrong with the flooring, such as a loose board or boards, many are unable confidently and quickly to remedy the situation. And what if boards need replacing, due to rot or wear?

Loose flooring

First, that loose floorboard—high on my list of minor faults—all that squeaking and groaning!

Take a look at the floorboard to ascertain why it moves. Perhaps it is no longer securely nailed to the joist, in which case the remedy is simple. Drive in another nail or so—for preference using a special floorboard nail. Perhaps the movement of the floorboard over the years has enlarged the hole round the nail, so that it no longer holds the board firmly. In that case, you can sometimes pull out the nail and insert a screw instead. But if pulling the nail out proves to be a difficult job then don't bother. Just drive in a screw close by, to hold the board firmly to the joist. Another cause could be that some sort of weakness has developed in a board—a crack, for instance—and as a result it will flex between joists, and rub against its neighbour. If you dust the area with french chalk or talcum powder, it should cure the squeak. Or wedge a thin lath between boards, to stop the movement.

However, it may not be the floorboards that are moving so much as the joists on which they are resting. Now there are four ways in which a joist can be fixed. It can be fitted into a socket left for that purpose in the brickwork of the walls—a method that is suitable for both ground and upper floors. On the ground floor, however, the joist may be resting on what is known as a sleeper wall—an extra low wall built inside the house and close to the main exterior wall. Upper floor joists may be supported on a wall plate (length of timber fixed to the wall) or else be carried in joist hangers—galvanized metal stirrups that are bedded into the brickwork mortar.

The remedy for a loose joist is to take up a section of the floor—you will probably have to take up at least two floorboards to give yourself enough room to work—and wedge the joist tightly into its socket or hanger (if that is the method of fixing) or nail it more securely to the sleeper wall or wall plate.

A word of warning

Before going on to how you take up a floorboard, I would like to refer back to the last section, where I mentioned driving a nail or screw into the board and joist. There is one big danger about driving nails and screws into floorboards. And that is the chance that there might be electricity cables or water or gas pipes underneath. The usual practice when these services are installed in the first place is to position them in the middle of the floorboard, so if you keep your nails and screws to the edges, then you ought to avoid them even if they are just below. But, of course, you can't always be sure.

Electricity cables do not present such a great risk as gas and water pipes, for they will usually pass low down through circular holes bored in the joist with some form of drill or brace. Rigid pipes, however, could never be fitted in this way, and for them notches are cut in the top of the joists. They are, therefore, right under the floorboards. So it is as well to try to work out whether there are any present or not.

How can you do this? Well, by trying to trace the course of the gas and water pipes in your home. If you have no gas laid on in the house, then obviously there will be no gas pipes to worry about. But if you do have gas, ask yourself whereabouts in the house it goes. Are there points in the bedrooms for gas fires, near the airing cupboard or the bathroom for a gas water heater, or just in the kitchen for a cooker? Then look at your gas meter and work out how the pipes will travel from there to the various points around your home.

Now try to trace the water system in the same way. Obviously, you are going to have a lot of water pipes in the bathroom and kitchen. There will be some, too, in a bedroom that has a wash-basin. Start from each tap and follow the pipes back as far as you can, for this will show you their likely route.

The room where you have to be particularly careful is one in which there is a central heating radiator, for there will be flow and return pipes to this.

Now, even with all the caution in the world, it is very easy to slip up. There is an old builders' saying that the only man who hasn't driven a nail through a water pipe is one who never nailed down a floorboard. So just in case you do have an accident let me tell you what to do. First turn off the water, then place a bucket in the room below to catch any drips. Now lift up the floorboard, so that you can get at the punctured pipe. Use a hacksaw to cut out 1 inch of pipework, centred on the hole. Now fit an ordinary compression joint, to link up the two cut ends, and you will have no more trouble. What is a compression joint, and how do you fit it? I explain all that in the chapter on plumbing—see page 18.

How to remove floorboards

Well, yes, there is a knack to this. First inspect the boards to see whether they are square edged, or have a tongue and groove. If you poke a knife blade in the gap between them you will soon be able to ascertain which type they are. The tongue of the board will have to be removed before it can be lifted, and if the boards are very close fitting so will the tongue of the neighbouring board that locates in the groove of the one you want to raise.

The tongue can be sawn off, or chopped off with the broad blade of an electrician's bolster. A long handsaw will be too unwieldy for this job, but you can usually manage it with a tenon saw, although the ideal tool is the tradesman's floorboard saw, which, unfortunately, you as a do-it-yourselfer are unlikely to have. Perhaps, however, you might be able to borrow one. A power saw can also be used, but set the blade so that it will only just penetrate through the tongue, thus minimising the risk of striking a power cable. Even so, there is the risk of hitting a nail, and damaging your saw. In very rare cases, the tongue may be a metal one, and you will then be faced with a lot of hard work with a hack saw blade. If a board has ever had to be raised before, then the tongues will already have been removed. For this reason it is always worth while trying to see if such a board is conveniently to hand.

Tools to use for prising up a board are the electrician's bolster, a claw hammer (preferably one with a ripping claw, which is set at a shallower angle than the conventional one), a very strong screwdriver, cold chisel, or old wood chisel. Begin at one end of the board and push whichever of these tools you will be using down the side of and under it, near the nails. Now start to lever up. In a very old board where movement has worn holes round the nails, you can sometimes punch these flush to the joists, to make your job easier. Gradually, the board will come free. Now you need a cold chisel, or something similar, and this is laid flat under the board, and resting on the two on each side of it. Push the cold chisel forward as far as it will go, and press with all your weight on the end of the board that is flapping free. This will tend to send a ripple down the whole length of board and free other nails, thus making your job of prising them out easier. Keep on in this way, pushing the cold chisel forward, and pressing down to cause ripples, until eventually you can lift up the whole board.

Sometimes, the board you need to raise may have no ends visible—i.e. it spans the whole length of the room, and disappears under the skirting board at each end—or perhaps one end may be showing. In that case you will have to create an end—or ends—artificially by sawing through the board at convenient points. You do this by making a starting hole with a drill, then sawing through with a pad saw. Obviously, you want to cut just through the floor-board, and not the joist as well. If you measure, roughly 1 inch from a set of nails, and drill there you will in most homes be well clear of the joist. But proceed carefully when making your drill hole, to make sure you are not boring into a joist or cable etc.

When you have to take up a board for any reason it is not a bad idea to look around and see if there are any services under the floor. Then you can make a note of them, ready for the next time you have to lift up boards in that room again.

At any rate, when you come to nail the boards back in place, there should be no chance of your hitting a pipe, because you look before you replace the board to see what you are nailing into.

I'll keep my fingers crossed for you! If the board you are replacing is one you have had to saw, then it will not be possible to nail it to a joist—you have sawn through it well clear of one, remember. In cases like this you have to screw short lengths of 2 × 1 inch timber on edge to the side joists, using a couple or so 2 or 3 inch nails. Then nail the board to these battens.

It is a good idea from time to time to inspect your floorboards, and replace any that are rotting, or defective in any way. If the reason for the defect appears to be woodworm, then have the whole area surveyed by a specialist firm. You can usually get this survey and an estimate for the work done free of charge.

5

Covering the floor with vinyl

MIKE SMITH

I mentioned in the earlier chapter on home insulation that the easiest way of stopping draughts coming up through gaps in your floorboards is to lay an all-over floor covering. But what is this covering to be?

One that would serve and is reasonably priced, is sheet vinyl. If you think of this as a cold, hard ,shiny material, then you are wrong. For the latest grades of vinyl incorporate a layer of resilient material that makes them soft and springy underfoot, warmer to the touch, and quieter to walk on. The surface is slightly textured, too, so that it is less slippery in places such as bathrooms. Furthermore, these vinyls have a softer sheen and a definite three-dimensional appearance that is very attractive. Cushionflor by Nairn is one example of such a vinyl.

Do not conclude from this that I feel the older, traditional type of vinyl does not have a place in home furnishing. It certainly does, for its hard-wearing, spill-resistant, easy-to-clean surface makes it an excellent floor covering in many parts of the home.

Vinyl first made its appearance in our homes in the shape of tiles, but sheet vinyl has so overtaken tiles in popularity that it now accounts for more than three-quarters of the vinyl sold. Add to its other qualities the fact that it is easy to lay, and you can see very clearly the reason why this is so.

Detailed instructions for laying this material may vary slightly from make to make, but this is how Nairn, at its floor laying school in Scotland, teaches tradesmen to lay vinyl.

The first job is to measure up your room and determine how

much vinyl you will need. You have to leave 3 inch wastage on each length, for trimming in, and you also need an allowance for matching-up patterns—just as you do when hanging wallpaper. Just how much this will involve depends on your pattern repeat, which could be anything from 6 inch to 18 inch. Working it all out can be quite complicated, so if you like you can give your supplier a plan of your room, and ask him to do it for you. Most will be only too happy to help you.

How to prepare the floor

Vinyl gives such an attractive surface that it is worth while getting rid of any imperfections in the floor on which it will be laid, to make sure they do not show through and mar the finished result. If the floor consists of boards, then punch all nail heads well home, and fix any loose boards, as I have described in Chapter 4. Next, it really is a good idea to line the floor with hardboard first. Yes, I know this is adding to the cost, but it will give you a more attractive floor to look at, and one that in the end will last longer. Rough floorboards and any with large gaps in between them certainly need covering but even where the boards are smooth and tightly fitting, the pattern of the planks can show through. In a lot of old books you may well see the advice to lay a paper underlay at right angles to the board. Well, don't you believe it. The experts have now decided it doesn't work.

As a do-it-yourselfer, you will probably find it easier to deal with 4 foot squares of hardboard than the standard 8×4 foot sheets that the tradesman would probably use. Lay them mesh side up, with their joints staggered—the sort of bonding effect you get with brickwork—nailing them at 4 inch centres round the edges, and at about 6 inch in the middle. If your work has not been too accurate, and you get gaps between the sheets and where they meet the wall, fill them up with cellulose filler.

Whenever you use hardboard, it is important to condition it first, but this is especially true for hardboard used as a flooring material. To condition hardboard you merely brush, or spray, three-quarters of a pint of water into the reverse side, then leave it stacked, mesh to mesh, in the room where it will be used for about 48 hours. This 48 hours is a fairly critical figure. It should not be any less than that, and certainly not much more. The point of this conditioning is that hardboard is a very absorbent material and this way its moisture content is brought up to a level to suit the room. If you did not do this, there might be a risk that the hardboard would twist and buckle, as it absorbed more moisture, or dried out.

If the floor is a solid one, the thing you have to determine is whether it is damp or not. Most vinyls should not be laid on damp floors.

How do you tell whether a floor is damp or not? Make this simple test. Take a 1 foot square sheet of metal (any kind as long as it is one that does not melt easily), and heat it on a gas cooker or with a blowlamp—better wear gloves whilst you do this. Then place the metal on the floor. If damp is present, then you will soon see a damp patch appearing on the floor, and "sweating" on the underside of the metal. If this first damp test is negative, try it in several parts of the room before giving the floor a clean bill of health.

What are you to do if the floor is damp? Well, there are certain types of vinyl that are not in themselves affected by rising damp, and you could use one of these. But, even so, you will get "sweating" underneath. No, really, the only thing to do is call in an expert to assess what is the cause, and what remedy is called for.

Actually, there are one or two do-it-yourself methods of damp-proofing a floor, and although the professional floor layer may shy away from them because he has to give his work a hundred per cent guarantee, often enough they do work. It's usually worth taking a gamble on them. Where a solid floor is not excessively damp and is reasonably smooth and level, there are various liquid membranes that you can brush on—your builders' merchant will sell them. These must be worked thoroughly into all cracks (in fact deep cracks are better filled with a levelling compound) and you then have a smooth surface on which to lay your sheet vinyl—or, in fact, any other type of floor covering.

Another way is to line the floor with hardboard or flooring grade chipboard, placing a sheet of 500 or 1,000 gauge polythene, or else a bituminous damp-proofing liquid underneath.

Does all this sound a lot of trouble? Well, of course, it is. But remember that, as well as protecting your floor covering, it will also be making the room dryer and warmer and altogether a healthier, pleasanter place to live in.

If you have a solid floor that is dry, you should still clean it before laying your vinyl—mop it down with a detergent. And, of course, any hollows should be filled with a floor levelling compound.

Laying the vinyl

The doorway into the room is as good a place as any to begin. Take the roll of material and cut a length 3 inch oversize. Place it vaguely in position, about 2 inch from the side wall, and riding up by roughly equal amounts into the doorway at one end of the length and up the opposite wall at the other.

Determine the greatest gap between the side wall and the edge of the vinyl, and cut a block of wood just slightly over this size. Now jam the block up to the wall, place a pencil hard against the block, and draw them along, tracing the contours of the wall on to the vinyl (picture 1). Thus you have a line to which you can cut, with either scissors, or a Stanley knife.

Now place the vinyl correctly in position against this side wall and scribe it to fit the end walls. It doesn't matter which of these you do first, but I will describe how you tackle the doorway end, since that is the most complicated. For the end scribing you need another block of wood, something like 3 or 4 inch long.

At any convenient point along the edge of the vinyl opposite the side wall, draw a pencil line that begins on the sheet and passes on to the floor (2). Now pull the sheet away from the doorway wall (3) by a distance equal to the length of your block of wood (4). Take the block, hold your pencil hard against it, and scribe the contours of the doorway wall onto the end of the length of vinyl, in exactly the same way as you marked those of the side all along one edge. As you work along the wall, you will come to the door frame. Follow the outline of this too (5) and then in the door opening scribe the vinyl to finish at a point halfway under the door when it is closed. Move on to the frame at the other side of the door opening and on to the wall beyond it. When you have finished you will once again have a line to which to cut. You should then have a perfect fit into the doorway opening and its adjacent wall (6).

Now follow exactly the same procedure at the other end of the length—i.e. with the vinyl in position against the side and doorway walls, make a pencil mark that also goes on to the floor, move the vinyl away from the wall by the length of your block of wood,

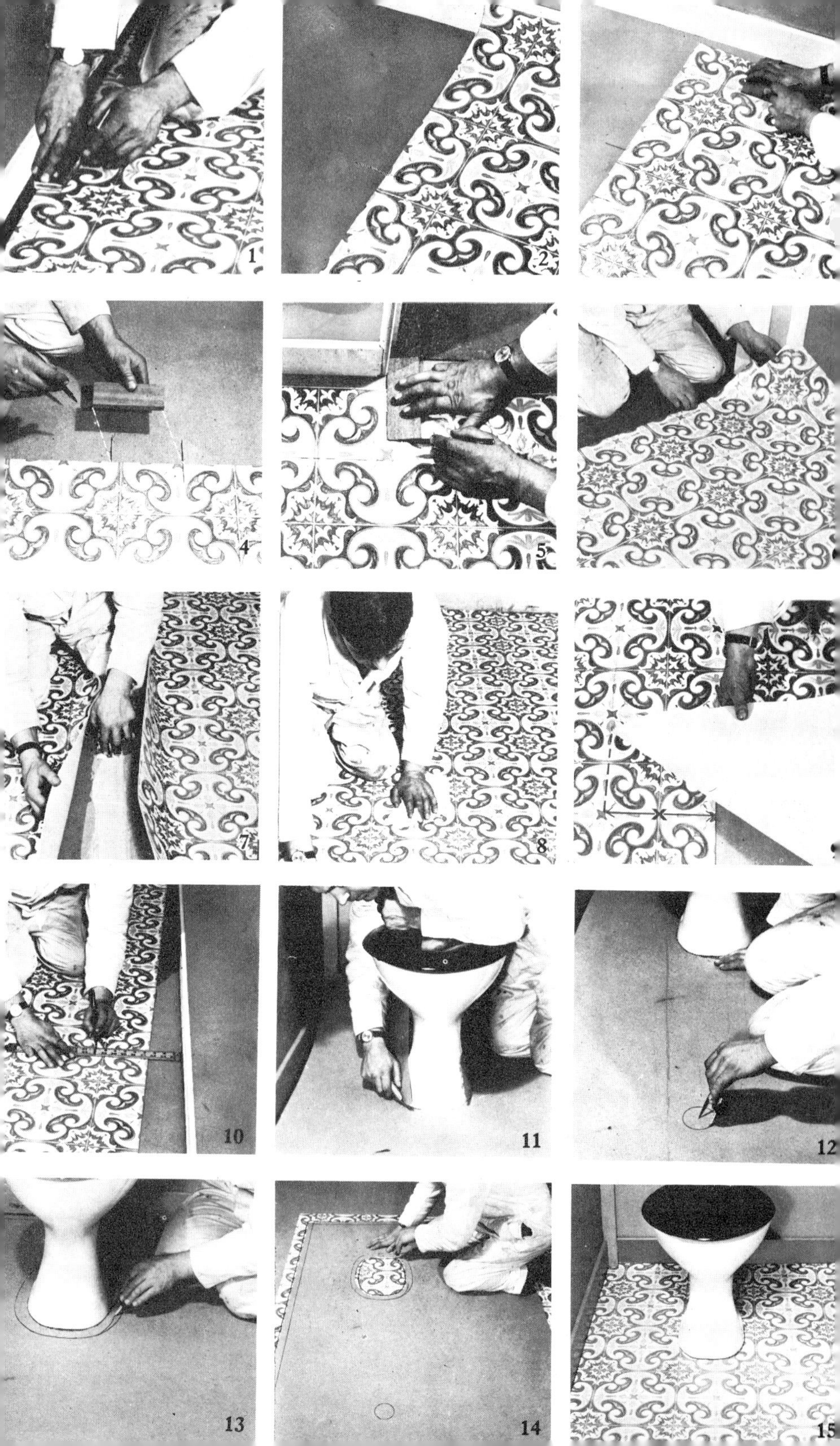

letting the sheet ride up the doorway wall. Then scribe it to the wall, and cut it to fit. With this first length in position, you are ready to fit its neighbour. Take the roll once more, pull out a length and match up the pattern as you would with wallpaper. Cut it to length, leaving just 1½ inch at each end for final trimming. Scribe the ends to the wall in the way already described.

The edges at the end of each length and the joins are stuck down (7)—but not the edges at each side of the room. Spread a 2 inch band of Copydex or similar material on to the floor, place the seams back in position, then rub them with a clean rag (8), using plenty of pressure to get a good bond.

Carry on laying lengths of vinyl until you come to the last one, which will inevitably have to be cut for width. Cut it first 3 inch oversize in length in the normal way, and place it on the floor, one edge overlapping its neighbour and positioned so that the patterns are true and parallel. Measure the overlap, then use a ruler with a pencil set at the same distance as the overlap away from the wall to scribe the contours of the side wall (10). Finally scribe this last piece to the end walls.

The most difficult job of all

But some rooms, of course, are so small that they can be covered in one piece. Such a room would be . . . well, the smallest room. And this has the complication of a lavatory to be fitted round. How do you cope?

Well, you need a pattern and either paper or felt will do for this. Line the floor with a piece of whatever pattern material you choose —the covering should not be made a perfect fit, but should be cut so that it is about 1 inch clear of the walls, and the w.c. (11). Now take a pair of compasses, and set these to a radius slightly larger than the widest gap between the paper and the wall. It is important that the compasses stay at the same setting throughout, and you might, of course, disturb them. Therefore, before you begin, draw a circle with them on the paper so that you can use this for a quick check-up any time you need (12).

Opposite: THE STEPS IN LAYING SHEET VINYL
(The numbers refer to the stages mentioned in the text)

Now place the point of the compasses against the base of the wall, and move them all round the room, tracing on the paper with the pencil the contours of the walls. Repeat the process round the lavatory (13), and any other obstructions. It is important throughout to keep the compasses perfectly at right angles to whatever is being scribed.

Thus you have drawn on the paper a line whose exact distance from every contour and obstacle in the room is the setting of the compass. So all you have to do is lift up the paper, place it on top of a sheet of vinyl cut very roughly oversize, put the point of the compasses on the pencil line on the paper, and follow this the whole way round. Keep the instrument perfectly at right angles, and it will trace on the vinyl a pencil line that will represent exactly the shape of the room, including obstructions such as the lavatory (14). Cut along this line with scissors or a knife and the vinyl should fit perfectly (15), although if you have slipped up at any point you might have to make minor adjustments here and there.

From the hole for the w.c., cut a straight line that will be hidden by the lavatory's pipework, and the sheet can then be fitted as one piece—a method you adopt for any obstacle in the middle of the room.

6

Fixing tiles to a wall

MIKE SMITH

There was a time when the job of fixing ceramic tiles to a wall was regarded as one of the most skilled in the building industry. But that was in the old days when tiles were large and thick, and they were fixed to the wall with sand and cement mortar. Now tile-fixing is a job that anyone, even a housewife who regards herself as completely unskilled in do-it-yourself, can manage. What has brought the change about? Two developments. First new easy-to-handle adhesives have made the mortar method obsolete, so that actually sticking the tiles to the wall is now simplicity itself. Secondly a whole range of ceramic tiles specifically designed for use by the do-it-yourselfer has evolved. Those from the H. & R. Johnson Cristal range, shown here, are typical. These are thinner than the traditional ones made for use by craftsmen, so it is much easier to cut them to size, and to fit round obstacles on the wall. Further, they have two little lugs on each edge, and these, although invisible in the final job, allow you to get an accurate spacing between each tile. For a neat evenly spaced dividing line between each tile, with all the lines straight and truly horizontal or vertical, is one of the hallmarks of a real craftsman's job. The spacer lugs make it easier for the amateur to scale those heights. In all other respects, do-it-yourself tiles are the equal of the thicker ones. They are just as hygienic, just as long-lasting, just as easy to clean.

If you have never tackled wall tiling before, you should begin with something simple—a few tiles round your kitchen sink, in a arder, or perhaps round your cooker. But maybe the best introduction to tiling would be to create a splashback over a washbasin. First decide what area ideally you would like the splashback to cover—you can draw on the wall with a pencil to help you. Now measure the area and place an order for the tiles—tiles are usually sold by area, rather than by number. When you get them home, measure the area they make up. Unless you have been inordinately lucky, you will probably find that you can make a splashback to the exact size of the one you wanted only by cutting some tiles. So if at all possible, change the size to one that can be made up from whole tiles. Re-draw the area and thoroughly clean the wall, removing any lumps or blisters. Small lumps can be got rid of with glasspaper; larger ones may need a scraper or a Surform tool. Now coat the entire area with adhesive, which is put on the wall, not on the tiles, and "comb" it with the serrated spreader supplied. This will form a series of ridges that ensure a better grip.

The adhesive will not hold the tiles immediately, and until it sets they will tend to slide down the wall. Therefore something has to be fixed to stop them. The top edge of the washbasin will serve but, if the tiling is to extend beyond the basin, you will have to fix a batten (2 × 1 inch is a suitable size) level with the basin and on each side of it. There is no need to bother about making a fixing with wall plugs; just drive ordinary nails through the battens and into the masonry.

Now start to place the tiles on the wall, taking care to position them accurately, locating them exactly on the spacer lugs. Complete the bottom row first, then go on to the second, and work your way up to the top. Some manufacturers sell round-edge tiles for the end of each row, and those at each end of the top row will need a round edge on two sides. Greater care than ever must be taken in positioning these, for they do not have spacer lugs. Other makers sell all their tiles with a slightly rounded edge, and, since they are so thin, no special tiles are called for.

The space you have left between the tiles is necessary, because ceramics are a living material and need room to expand and contract. But the gap cannot be left open. For not only would it look unsightly, but also it would be a collecting ground for dirt and germs. The material used to fill it in is very similar to the adhesive, and is known as grout; you buy it when you get the tiles. Once the adhesive has set, you can apply the grout. Push it well into the joints using a sponge. Any that gets on to the face of the tiles should be wiped off with a damp cloth or sponge before it can set. Then, for the best finish, take a pointed stick and draw it along each joint. Finally, give the tiles a good polish with a dry cloth, remove the battens, and you have finished your first exercise in tiling.

Of course, it may not be possible for you to make a splashback without cutting some tiles; there just may not be sufficient room. In that case do not worry, for cutting the thin do-it-yourself tiles just is not difficult. Use a proper tiler's spike—do not be persuaded to try a wheeled glass cutter. Take a straightedge—a ruler is ideal, but a short length of wood that is truly square will do instead—and place it on the face of the tile, where you want to cut it. Draw the spike firmly across the face holding it against the straightedge. Be sure that you cut right through the glaze, and not only that on the face, but on the edges, too. Avoid making a series of strokes that will give you more than one cut. Now place the tile on a table or bench, so that the score mark coincides with the edge, and the waste portion overhangs. Hold the tile with one hand, and press hard on the waste with the other. It should then break cleanly along the line. Oh yes, you will have trouble at first, but eventually you will acquire the knack. Make sure, though, you tell your supplier to give you one or two extra tiles so that you can practise on them.

When you are doing any job that uses cut tiles, you must make sure that you set out your work nicely. The cut tiles at the end of each row (yes, you have to cut two, not one, because each row may well end with a round edge, remember; and even if it does not a cut tile at just one end would not look neat) should be of equal size. So mark the centre of the bottom row and set out a trial row to find out which will give you the neatest arrangement—one tile on each side of the centre line, or one tile placed centrally on it.

This setting-out of work for the neatest and most attractive effect is one of the most important aspects of the tiler's craft, and it assumes special importance if your first efforts at tiling encourage you to go on to tackle a whole wall.

But for such a job you must first make sure that the wall surface is suitable. As well as being clean, dry and free from bumps, it also needs to be level across its whole surface, or the tiles will not lie flat and true against each other. If your wall is not in good condition it needs to be lined first with hardboard and the fact that you have to do this may well deter you from tackling such a job. However, here's what is involved.

The hardboard is pinned to a framework of battens that should be about 2 inch wide and of the same thickness as the skirting board, for you may well be able to use the skirting as part of the framework. You need a batten at the edge of every board and at 2 foot intervals in addition to that. Thus, for standard 8 × 4 foot boards placed vertically, you would screw into wall plugs a vertical batten at 2 foot centres from floor to ceiling, then a series of separate cross battens, between each vertical one, again at 2 foot centres.

Now comes the tricky bit. It is no use screwing these battens firmly in place for they would then follow the contours of the wall and you would have gone to all that trouble merely to reproduce a surface similar to the one you were trying to get rid of. So you must use a long wooden straightedge, and a spirit level, to make sure that all the members are truly vertical and in plane with each other. This will entail a lot of slackening off of screws, placing packing of card or thin timber under the batten at one point, and tightening up of others at another point. When you are satisfied that the battens are accurately fixed, you can pin the hardboard to it, then start to tile.

You cannot use the skirting board, even if you have not covered it up, or the floor if there is no skirting, as a guide for the tiles, because both of them may well be out of true. So tack a batten in place, just as you did for the splashback, but this time one that runs the whole length of the wall, its top edge one tile's height from the lowest point of the floor or skirting board. Check with a spirit level that it is truly horizontal.

To help you with the setting-out, which will be a little more complicated than for the simple splashback, you should make a measuring staff. This is simply a lath on which you make a series of marks, each one equal to the full width of the tile, including its spacer lugs. Now mark the centre of the batten you have tacked to the wall and, working from this point, use the measuring staff to show which arrangement of tiles would be the neatest. There are two possibilities. You can begin with one tile each side of the centre line, or one placed centrally on it. Your measuring staff will indicate which of these alternatives would give you the largest cut tile at each end of the row, and that is the one you should adopt.

You may wonder why it is necessary to make the measuring staff, and whether it would not be simpler to mark the size of the tiles on the wall batten. The answer is that you would have to make two sets of marks (one for each of the two possible settings out) on each batten, of which, of course, there would be more than one, if you were fully tiling every wall in the room.

The tiles must be not only vertically, but also horizontally, true, so drop a plumb line at the point where the last uncut tile and one end of the bottom row will finish and mark the line on the wall with pencil. Now, working from this point, apply adhesive to about a square yard of the wall and fix the tiles in place one at a time. Work from the bottom, using the wall batten and the plumb line to make sure everything is true. Then deal with another square yard to the side of the first, and soon, when you have covered the whole bottom section of the wall, deal with a section higher until it is all finished. In the first instance, though, placc only whole tiles in position, so that you will be left with a margin at each side and at the top. Try not to get any adhesive on this gap. The cutting of all the tiles to size can now be tackled at one go, but measure for each individually. Because the walls will not be perfectly true, you cannot assume that each cut tile will be the same size. Stick the tile on the wall as soon as you have cut it, so that you do not get the various pieces mixed up, and for such small tiles the adhesive should not be spread on the wall, but "buttered" on the back of the tile.

If you need an L-shaped tile, to go round some obstruction, mark it in the usual way by scoring with your spike held firmly against a straightedge, but avoid making any of the legs of the L too long, or you will get a cross-shape and these marks will mar the finished job. Snip out the waste with a pair of pincers. Final trimming can be done with an ordinary carpenter's rasp. Round holes, which are needed when you come up against a pipe, for instance, can have the main body of the waste snipped out with pincers, and the round back of a rasp will once again finish off the shaping. Do not, however, try to cut a hole (round or square) in the middle of a tile. Cut the tile in two, approximately across where the centre of the hole would be, and cut half of the hole in one edge of each of the two half tiles.

If you have to tile round a washbasin in the bathroom, work to the nearest full tile both on top and on each side and support the tiling above with a wall batten, using your spirit level to make sure it is horizontal. Window and door frames should be treated in just the same way. If a doorway is placed inside an opening, a wall batten will be needed over it to stop the tiles sliding down the wall, and inside the opening round-edge tiles will have to be used where the tiles inside the opening meet those on the wall. Ordinary tiles are used and cut to size to finish off the rest of the opening. Tiles fixed to the top underside of an opening should not come crashing to the floor if you press them firmly in place, but to make sure you can cut a piece of plywood to the size of the opening and prop it up hard under the tiles, so that it will hold them, by wedging two long lengths of 2 inch square timber between the plywood and the floor.

When the glue of the main body of the tiling has set, you can remove all the various lengths of wall batten, and cut tiles to fit the space left. Then fill with grout, just as described for the splashback.

As you carry out the final polishing of the tiles, and pause to admire the splendid job you have made of your tiling, you may well ask yourself why so many tradesmen still stick to the old size of tile. Really, I don't know the answer to that either. I can only presume it is the notorious conservatism of the building industry at work again.

Opposite: THE STEPS IN TILING A WALL

1. Checking that the wall is horizontal.
2. Making a measuring staff.
3. Checking that the tiles will be truly vertical.
4. Applying adhesive to the wall.
5. Fixing the tiles in place.
6. Scoring with a tiler's spike.
7. Snipping out an L-shape.
8. A batten supports tiles round a washbasin . . .
9. . . . and above a window or door opening.
10. Finally applying the grout.

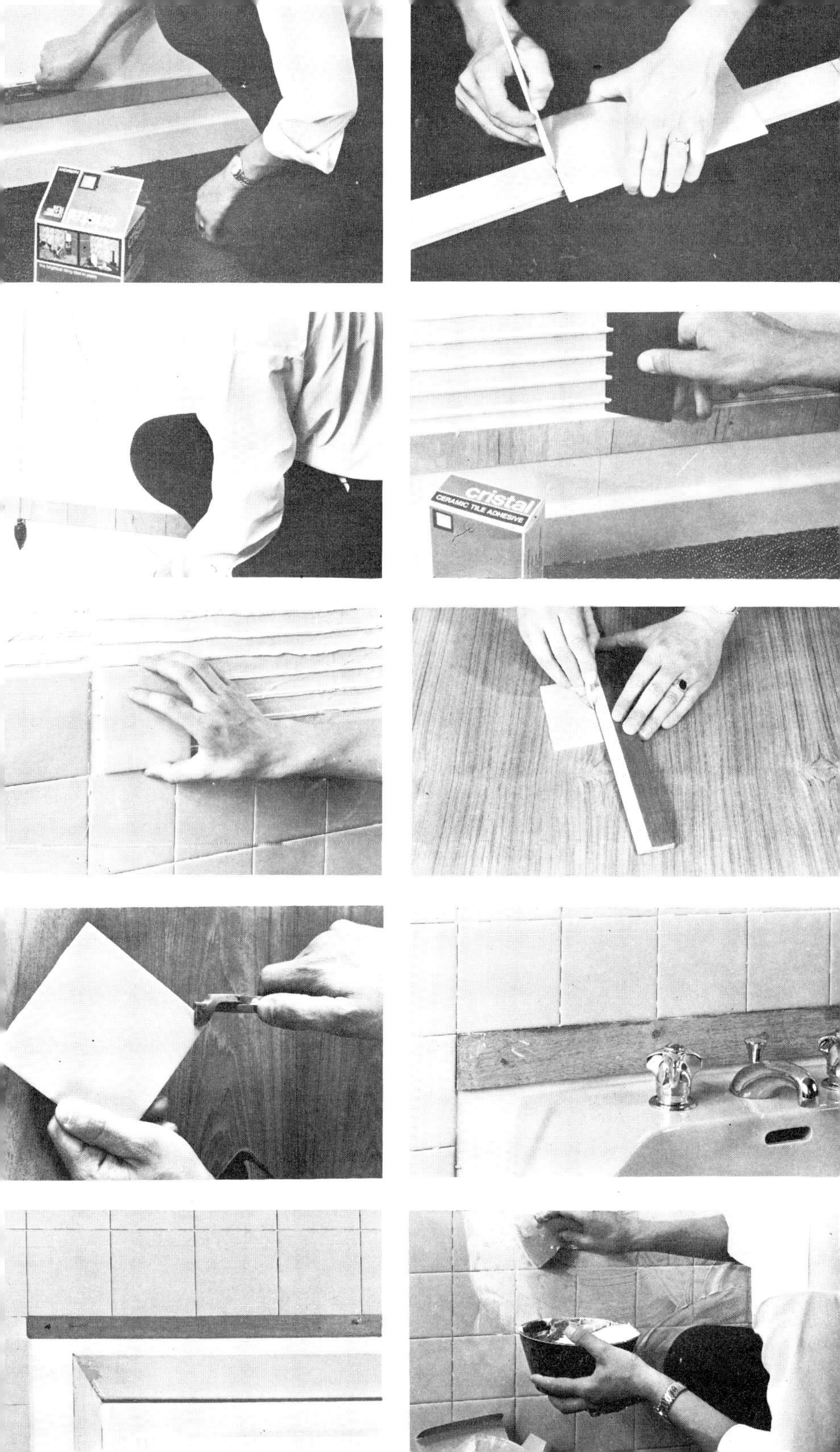
cristal
CERAMIC TILE ADHESIVE

7

Something about windows

MIKE SMITH

There is, as many people have discovered, one easy way to modernise the external appearance of an old house. And that is to make its windows larger. The trend ever since the war has been to bigger windows, and ultra-modern houses have enormous stretches of glass. Therefore, if only you can take your tired looking tatty old house and give it bigger windows, it will look more up to date. That, at any rate, is the theory and there is certainly a lot in it.

But I do hope you will consider with discretion any such scheme you may have in mind. For the windows of a house are part of its character. Change them unsympathetically, and you destroy that character. For instance, it would not be right to see an olde worlde West Country thatched cottage with huge picture windows. And the small panes of the Georgian sash window are part of the appeal of that elegant style of building. Yet there is no doubt that a lot of the nondescript houses, built between the wars, for instance, do look better with larger windows, instead of a lot of fussy little panes. Even here, however, I think that from a design point of view you ought to be a little cautious, and relate whatever plans you have to the overall appearance of your house, and its neighbours. Otherwise the whole effect looks like nothing so much as a toothless grin.

With those reservations in mind, however, I want to say that I am all in favour of streamlining the windows of your house, and in fact I have done precisely this in my own home. Anyway, apart from the look of the thing, there is the enormous bonus

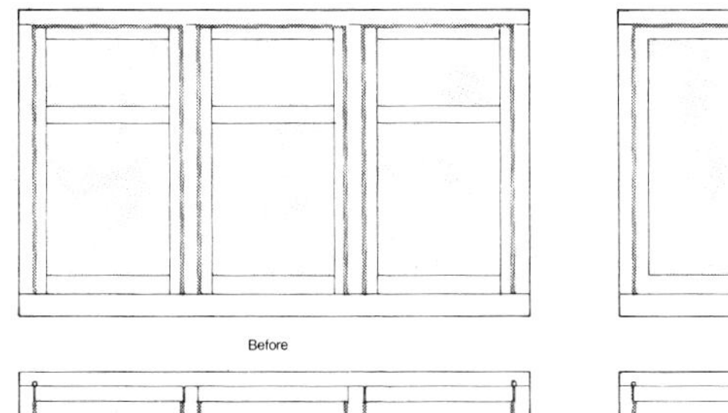

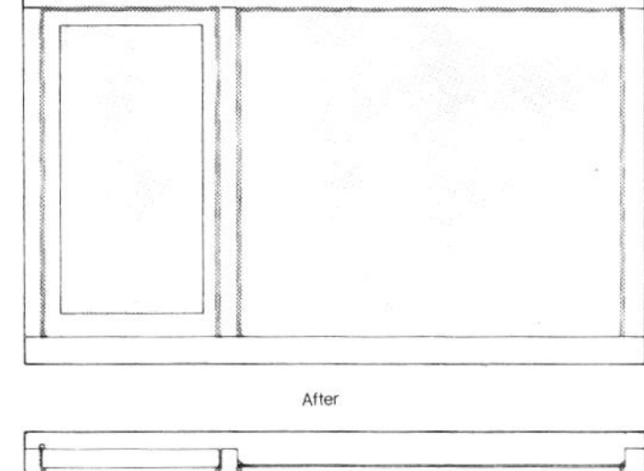

How to modernise old windows.

you get of extra light. You wouldn't think that the removal of a few fairly narrow pieces of timber would have all that much effect, but the difference in brightness after the conversion has been carried out amazes most people.

In my sketch here, I show the typical window of a house of the thirties ripe for such treatment, with a suggested "after". The window consists of three parts. That on the left is a hinged casement, whilst the other two are fixed sashes. In addition each part has a horizontal bar dividing the sash into a large bottom and a smaller top section.

There will be many small different design points about various windows but basically this is what you do. The sashes will be nailed into rebates in the main frame, so you just stand on the inside of the room, then use a mallet or hammer and a piece of wood to tap away at the sash until eventually you knock it clean out. In the type of window I show here, one large sash may stretch from top to bottom of the frame, or there may be a large complete sash below, with a smaller one on top. But in any case the principle is the same.

Knock out in this way all the individual sashes that you wish to remove. You will then still be left with one or two frame members in the way of the design you are aiming for. These you saw off as close to the frame as possible. That will leave you with just the stubs of the frame members to remove to give you a rebate ready to receive the glass. You will be able to get rid of the stubs with just a saw in some cases, but in others you may have to use a chisel or a plane or Surform.

When you have done this, clean out the rebate generally with a chisel and sandpaper, (snipping out any nails left in) and it is ready to receive the glass.

Glazing

When you are ordering the glass, tell your supplier what it is for, because the bigger the window, the thicker will your sheet of glass have to be. Normally 24 oz. glass is used; but, for windows above average sizes, 32 oz. is used for panes up to 5×4 foot, and float or plate glass for larger than this.

As for size, the glass should be $\frac{1}{16}$ inch all round less than the opening. You will also buy your putty from the glazier, and he should be able to tell you how much you will need for the size of window you are dealing with.

Take some putty and roll it into a ball large enough to grasp in the palm of your hand. If the putty is stiff and hard to work, you can add linseed oil. Now hold the ball of putty in your hand, and squeeze it between your thumb and forefinger into the rebate.

When the whole of the rebate is covered with putty, you can put the pane of glass in position. This will probably be heavy enough for you to need a helper. Press the glass into place, applying pressure only at the edges. Not only will this be more effective in pushing the glass home, but also there is less chance of your breaking the window than if you pushed it in the middle. Your aim should be to ensure that there is about $\frac{1}{16}$ inch of putty between the back of the glass and the rebate.

The glass is held in place by glazing sprigs—a type of nail—which are hammered into the frame at 9 inch centres. It is obviously not an easy job wielding a hammer so close to the glass without breaking it, but you should use a smallish Warrington hammer and tap the sprig with the pene—the part of the head opposite the face. Otherwise use the blade of an old chisel.

Now more putty is applied to the face of the glass to ensure a waterproof seal. Once again, the professional glazier would kneed the putty into a ball and squeeze it into place. If you find this too difficult, you can roll it into worms and press it in place with a knife.

The putty needs to be bevelled, both to give a good appearance and to ensure that rainwater will run off it. The bevelling is done with a knife, and you should take care to do this properly. Try to get an even bevel all the way round, and one that is equal to that on neighbouring panes. Pay particular attention to a good mitred finish at the corners—you will probably find it easiest to work away from these. The top of the bevel incidentally should be below the level of the putty inside the room.

When the bevel is finished you can go indoors, and use the knife to trim off the excess putty. The putty, of course, needs to be protected from the weather by paint (use a primer followed by an undercoat and two top coats) but wait a couple of weeks before doing this, to give the putty time to dry out.

Your only job now is to persuade little boys not to play football in front of your house, because now you have a bigger pane, the cost of repairing a smashed one will be so much higher in future.

Sash windows

There is, however, another problem you might have with windows, and that is making the very old fashioned kind—sliding sashes—function properly. Before you can begin to do this, you must first of all understand how they work. In talking about this type of window, I want to use the correct term that is applied to each part of the system, and, so that you will be able to understand me more clearly, I have labelled each of the parts in the accompanying sketch.

The window system consists of two sashes that slide up and down, each in its own groove. The outer window is the one that is normally at the top, and the inner one should be at the bottom when both sashes are closed. Some sort of catch is usually fixed to lock the two of them together. The grooves in which they slide are formed by three beads—the outer is known as the stop bead, the middle as the parting bead, and the inner as the staff bead.

A system of counter-balancing weights is used to ensure that the sashes will remain in whatever position they are left when the windows are pushed up and down. The weights are in hidden compartments out of view, and they are attached to cords which pass over a pulley high up in the sides of the window frame and are then fixed by tacks to the sides of the sashes. The fixing point is usually in a groove in the side of the sash, so that the cord does not protrude and stop the sashes from fitting fairly snugly against the side of the frame.

Access to the weight compartment is by means of a fillet of timber called a pocket that is a push fit in an opening in the side

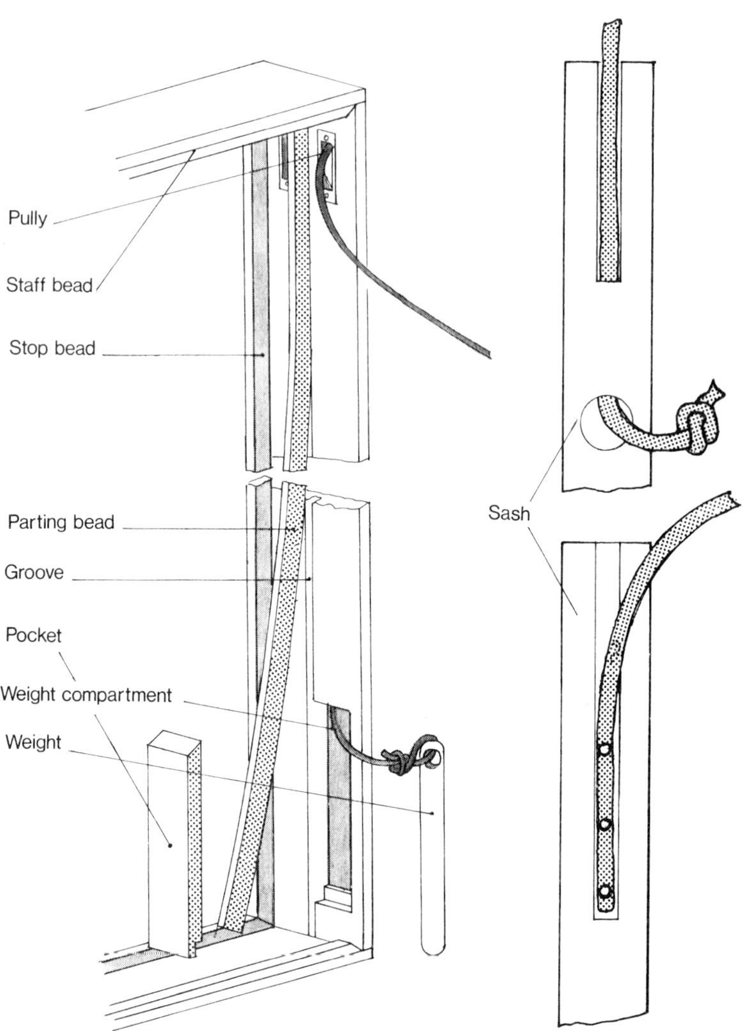

The parts of a sliding sash window.

of the frame.

That seems a very simple system, and so it is. What can go wrong? Well, quite a few things. One common fault is that the sashes will not slide properly—they seem to stick, and get jamme l. You can try rubbing soap or candle grease into the grooves—just as you would for a drawer that is sticking—but this will produce a cure in only a minority of cases. For the trouble is likely to go deeper than that, and there are two possible causes.

In the first place, the beads may have been removed at some time and replaced too near the sashes, which as a result do not have enough room to manoeuvre. In that case, the beads must be prised off, and re-positioned correctly. Taking them off is easy, for they are merely pinned in place and glue is not, and never should be, used. You just push an old screwdriver or chisel between the bead and the frame and lever the bead clear. Take care when you nail the beads back that you do not go to the other extreme and put them too far away, otherwise the sashes will rattle and you will get strong draughts.

In fact, strong draughts and rattling sashes are another fault that does develop. The remedy is similar. You take off the beads and re-position them, this time taking care not to put them too near, or else a jammed window will be the result.

But back to sticking sashes. The other likely cause is that there may be too big a build-up of paint inside the grooves. Over the years, each time the room has been painted, yet another coat—perhaps even two or three—will have been slapped on to the frame without any thought having been given to stripping off old paint. This will have increased the thickness of the beads, and cut down on the depth of the groove considerably. As a result, there just will not be enough room for the sashes to slide.

The remedy for this is quite simple. You must strip off the paint down to the bare wood, using either a blowlamp or a chemical stripper. Then re-paint, starting off with a primer, followed by an undercoat, and finishing off with one or two top coats.

Of course, it will be impossible to wield a blowlamp in the grooves without burning through the cords, not very convenient to use a chemical stripper and difficult to use a paint brush without getting paint all over the cords. Therefore, I think it is well worth while to remove the sashes entirely before you start work, especially as it is not a very difficult process to do so.

How to remove a sash

The sashes are held in position just by the beads and once those are prised out (as already described) the sashes themselves can be swung clear. First lift out the staff or inner beads, the inner sash can now swing clear and you will be able to get at the cord in the grooves. Remove the nails holding the cord on one side. This can be done with a small claw hammer, pliers or pincers. A very handy tool, however, is a tack lifter. This in appearance is not unlike a screwdriver, except that the tip of the blade is much wider, and there is a V-cut in it. The blade is slipped under the head of a tack or nail, then you give a quick jerk, and the tack should be freed and capable of being lifted clear. One thing you have to be wary of is the cord being pulled over the pulley and down into the weight compartment. Therefore, keep hold of it until you get the chance to tie a very big knot in the end of it, so that it will merely jam up against the top of the pulley.

Now deal with the cord on the other side in just the same way and the inner sash can be lifted clear. To remove the outer sash, you merely prise off the parting bead (you will notice, incidentally, that this is fixed inside a groove) and free the cords in just the same way.

Whenever you remove any of the beads it is a good idea to take a close look at them and see whether it is worth while putting them back. Over the years they can rot and wear out and the strain they were subjected to in being prised out may well have been the last straw. Replacement beads are very easy to buy, particularly from suppliers in the inner suburbs of our large towns where there are a lot of houses with sash windows. If you do buy new ones, you will, of course, be spared the task of stripping the paint off the old ones.

All the work of stripping off the old paint and applying three or four coats of new can obviously not be done in one day, and yet you will not want to leave that gaping great hole in your window when you go to bed. It might rain during the night and, anyway, you will be encouraging burglars or stray animals to come indoors. There is, however, no need to go to all the fuss of replacing the beads and the sash cords. Put the outer sash back in place, in either a closed or open position, and nail it to the stop bead. Put the inner sash in place and nail it to the outer sash. Do not drive these nails fully home, so that you can easily withdraw them when you come to start work again. You may say that this is not very secure, and you would be right. But anyone who tried to push the sashes inwards would cause such a noise that it would waken the whole neighbourhood up.

When you come to put everything back permanently, you must be sure that the cords are firmly nailed in place, otherwise the sashes could work loose and come crashing down, breaking a lot of glass. And you must once again take great care that you position the beads properly.

Broken sash cords

One final piece of maintenance you might have to carry out is replacing a broken sash cord. Symptoms indicating the need for this will be that it is very hard work to raise the windows—the weights will not be counterbalancing to help you—also, the window will not stay in a raised position. And the evidence of a broken cord should be there before your very eyes.

Once again, remove the beads and lift out the sashes. Get rid of whatever debris of cord is still attached in the grooves. Next you must prise out the pocket of the weight compartment—I have already explained that this is just a push fit, so an old chisel or screwdriver will easily do this. Put your hand inside the compartment, lift the weight out and get rid of any old cord still attached to it.

Now take some new cord and cut it to the correct length. It is important that this is fairly accurate. The length should be such that the window can be fully raised, without the weight starting to touch the floor of its compartment (if it did that, it could not be counterbalancing) and the window must be capable of being fully lowered, without the weight jamming up against the back of the pulley.

Tack one end of the cord into the groove of the sash. Now you need what builders call a mouse. This is a length of thin string to one end of which is attached a tiny weight. This can be anything so long as it is small enough to pass over the pulley and into the box, yet heavy enough to pull the string down to the bottom of the compartment.

Push the mouse into the weight compartment, and let it fall down, but making sure that enough string is left hanging outside at the other end. Tie this string to the free end of the cord you have nailed to the sash, put your hand inside the weight compartment, take hold of the end of the mouse dangling inside, pull gently, drawing the cord over the pulley. Once it is inside the compartment, you can tie it to the weight. This is your final chance to correct the length of the cord. Push the pocket back in place and the repair is complete.

Whilst you are mending one cord that has broken, it is worth your while looking at all the other cords in the same window—and for that matter the cords in other windows—for a cord can fray suddenly and cause a window to come crashing down, perhaps with the risk of breaking some glass.

Finally, every so often it is worth while putting a little bit of oil on the pulleys (but not so much that you get it all over the frame) so that they run more freely and do not squeak so much.

8

Removing an old fireplace

MIKE SMITH

When you take over a new house, the most important fixture you will be left with in every room, visually at any rate, will be the fireplace. You can bring in your own furniture, carpets, curtains, paint the woodwork in colours that are your choice, hang wallpaper that pleases you. But all the time you will be left with a fireplace that someone else thought attractive. Why not get rid of it, so that you will then be able to create a style of decor that pleases you?

But first I would like to warn you against being too destructive. An old fireplace is sometimes a thing of beauty in its own right, and it can be quite valuable, too. Here I am not talking merely about the antique masterpieces that people travel miles to see in our famous country homes. No, as an example, the old fashioned cottage kitchen range, which the middle-aged reader may well have seen his mother or grandmother use to cook the family dinner, is now being prized as a collector's piece. But a lot of nondescript fireplaces have been installed in our homes, especially during the thirties, and good riddance to these, say I.

Taking out a factory-made fireplace, which has been installed as one piece, is easy. It will have little metal lugs each side of it and screws will pass through holes in the lugs into plugs in the wall. All you have to do is locate the lugs, withdraw the screws, prise out the fireplace and lift it away.

Finding the lugs should not be too difficult. They will, of course, be hidden under the plaster, so what you have to do is take a hammer and, preferably, a cold chisel, although you could I

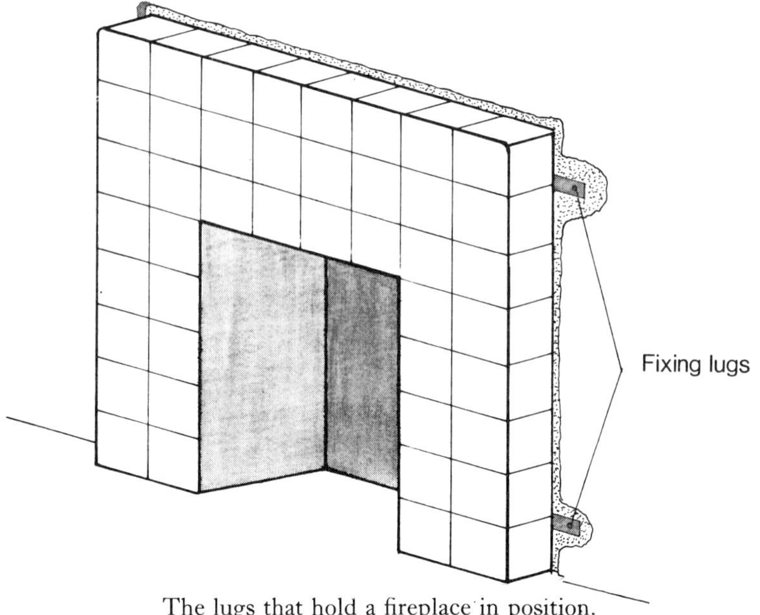

The lugs that hold a fireplace in position.

suppose make do with an old carpentry chisel. Now tap all the way round the edge of the fireplace sides until you see the lugs. You can normally expect to find two on each side of the fireplace although there may sometimes be more—occasionally you may come across some along the top edge. Use a screwdriver to withdraw the screws. Usually the fireplace can now just be lifted clear, although in some cases plaster and/or cement may still be lightly bonding it in place. In this case, it will need to be prised out but this should not be difficult. Obviously, though, the fireplace will be heavy, so you should get assistance. People with weak backs or muscles should take particular care. An ordinary, humdrum fireplace is now fit only to be smashed up and used as rubble. But, as I said earlier, beware of what you are destroying.

The hearth will often merely be resting in place on a concrete slab, incorporated into the fabric of a sprung-timber floor, although in many instances cement might have been used to bond it in position. All you have to do is tap gently with hammer and cold chisel to break whatever bond exists, then ram a crowbar, or even a strong garden spade, underneath the hearth to raise it.

You will notice that I have so far been talking about factory-made fireplaces, and these are in the majority of cases the only ones you will come across. It does sometimes happen, though, that you meet a fireplace that has been built *in situ*, as for instance by brick being laid on brick, or tiles stuck directly to a wall. Such a thing is possible, for instance, if you are moving into a house once owned by an enthusiastic do-it-yourselfer. In such cases, the only course open to you is to demolish the fireplace bit by bit, once again using a cold chisel and a heavy hammer.

I hope for your sake you do not have to remove such a fireplace, for what would otherwise have been a clean straightforward job becomes messy and time-consuming, although there is the bonus that you will not have the back-breaking job of carrying the fireplace outside in one piece.

Putting in the new fireplace

Now . . . what do you have in mind? Putting in a new purpose-built fireplace that is more to your taste? If it is a fairly modern one you have taken out, then your job should not be too difficult. If you can get one with a suitably sized fire-opening, then the new fireplace goes in just as the old one came out. You might have to chip off extra plaster if the new one is much bigger, and since the retaining lugs will almost certainly not be in exactly the same place, you will have to drill holes and insert wall plugs to receive the screws. But that is all. Mix up a bit of plaster (or cellulose filler for small areas) to repair any ravages in the wall rendering and the job is done.

Of course, you might not be content merely to use a manufactured fireplace and you might want something more individual instead. For instance, you might want to build your own stone fireplace and there is no reason why you shouldn't. But remember that stone is very heavy material and you want to be sure the floor will be able to support the weight of the new fireplace. If you are building one just around the chimney breast, then you are not likely to have any problems. And if your room has a solid concrete floor, then it doesn't matter, anyway. But you should not carry stone across a timber floor supported on joists, unless an expert has vetted it to make sure it is strong enough, or else the joists have been shored up—a job for a builder.

Your first step is to mark out with chalk the area of the fireplace

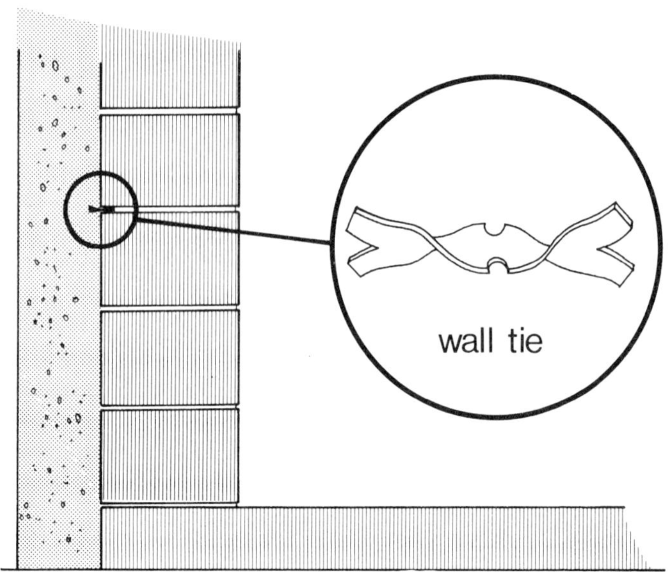

Metal ties are needed to strengthen a stone fireplace.

on both the floor and the wall. The fireplace is built by means of simple bricklaying—i.e. you lay one stone on top of another, and bond them together with a mortar of four parts of soft sand to one of cement. There should be a layer of bituminous felt between the floor and the first course of stones and a layer of mortar is spread on the felt.

In addition, to stop the fireplace from falling forward, metal ties are used every three courses, and at each corner. The ties should be about $6 \times 1\frac{1}{2} \times \frac{1}{8}$ inch and you chop out holes in the chimney breast to receive them. The ties are then cemented into the holes and in a course of stonework.

Begin by laying a largish block at each corner of the fireplace, then another largish one each side of the fireplace opening. Carry on laying the courses—these can be random or regular as you wish—checking frequently with a plumb line and bob that the corner is vertical and using a spirit level to make sure the courses are truly level. Mortar should be used on the back of the stone as well as between the horizontal and vertical joints.

Across the top of the fire opening you will need a lintel, which can be a stone block that is long enough, or a bar of $3 \times \frac{3}{8}$ inch steel, overlapping the opening by 6 inch at each end. Then carry on "bricklaying" in the normal manner above this.

What do you have in mind as a mantleshelf? Slate or stone are possible materials and these are bedded in mortar. Or you might fancy a length of attractive hardwood. Note, however, that no timber should ever be nearer than 9 inch to the fire itself. One easy way of fixing this is to drive a few screws into the underside of the hardwood, but leave them projecting about ½ inch. Then lay the wood on a bed of mortar, tapping it down so the screw heads sink well in. When the mortar sets it will grip them tightly and the wood will never move. But whatever you choose for a mantleshelf, it is important that it be level, so check with a spirit level.

When you come to do the hearth, chalk out its area on the floor and cement your stone in place. Once again, because of the weight problem, it is not advisable to carry the stone much beyond the concrete slab—and, in fact, not at all, if you have reason to doubt the soundness of the floor. To make sure you get the hearth level, place a piece of wood over it, and put a spirit level on the wood. You should border off your hearth with a raised "kerb" of taller stones.

Where, incidentally, do you buy the stones? They are sold at many specialist outlets and often at garden centres. Then you have to adopt a sort of jigsaw puzzle technique, to make up an attractive looking fireplace. As an alternative, kits for building stone fireplaces can be bought.

Stone is not the only "outdoor" material that can be used for fireplaces. Brick is also popular with some people, and here the technique is just the same, except that you do not have the problem of matching up different sized components. Or you can use slate. In this case, it is not a matter of bedding slabs on top of each other, but of facing a wall. Kits are available that use a system of special hooks for attaching the slates and holding them in place.

Instead of a fireplace . . . what?

So far, I have been assuming that you would want a working fireplace—one in which it is possible to burn coal. But that might not be the case. You might be thinking of going over to another form of fire—gas or electric. Now you must not put a combustible material close to the flame or flue of a gas fire, but it is possible to devise an attractive setting for your gas fire by covering the whole of the former fireplace position with a sheet of asbestos, for example. You paint the parts of this that will show (but keep paint well away from the flue at the back) and edge the sheet with an attractive hardwood.

A similar arrangement can be devised for an electric fire but this time you need not be quite so fussy about fire risk. You can use timber or timber-based materials (hardboard, plywood, chipboard etc.) to hide the ravages left by your removal of the old fireplace.

You must also ask yourself whether you want a fireplace at all. Certainly, the bedroom fireplace is redundant today and fireplaces can even be regarded as superfluous in living rooms of homes that use electric fires exclusively, or are centrally heated. For remember that a fireplace, including its hearth, takes up a lot of space in a small room.

So what goes in place of the fireplace? Well, it could be just nothing. The fireplace opening can be bricked up, the bricks plastered over, new skirting board fixed in place, and there you are. But if you think that an unskilled amateur who has never plastered before can skim over a bricked-up fireplace opening and make it look as though there never has been a fireplace there at all, then I am afraid you are in for an unpleasant shock. In fact, from what I see on my rounds I should say that such skill is beyond many tradesmen these days. For plastering is the most difficult job in the building industry, and really top-rate plasterers are very rare. So I am afraid that, for the plastering, you will have to call in an expert.

But the bricking-up you can most certainly do yourself. For this, I suggest you use not bricks, but building blocks, which are much easier for the amateur to handle. You can even cut them with a saw—not one with which you expect to do some fine carpentry work later on, but the tougher all-purpose saws, and even a hacksaw. Bed a layer of mortar, of 3 parts of sand to 1 of cement, on the floor of the opening, and lay your first course of blocks on this, cutting the last one to fit. Now start the second course, laying them in a bond so that the joints are staggered. Carry on like this until the whole opening is blocked up.

The hardest part of fitting the skirting board will be buying stuff to match that already in the room. This can present a real problem, especially in an old house with very deep ornate stuff. In more modern homes there should not be the same trouble, and you should be able to buy something suitable, although a few strokes of your plane might be needed to make it a perfect match. All you do is cut the board to length, nail it in place using cut nails, which will easily penetrate the building blocks and use cellulose filler to disguise the points where it joins the short lengths of skirting that was there previously.

There is, of course, one other way of disguising an old fireplace opening, and one that gets round the problem of bricklaying, finding a good plasterer, matching-up skirting—the lot. That is to fit some sort of built-in unit over the opening. The unit could take the form of a bedhead or built-in dressing table in a bedroom, or some form of bookshelf or wall unit in a living room—the possibilities are endless.

The chimney flue

But whatever way you disguise the fireplace opening, there is still the problem of the flue. Unless you take care, this will become a place where dank air is trapped and you could introduce damp into your chimney breast, with the tell-tale signs showing through to stain your decorations. There are two things you can do to avoid this. Firstly, in the old fireplace opening, you can fit a grille, which can either be cemented into your building blocks, or screwed to a unit made of wood. You will need different types of grille according to which method you adopt, so when you go to buy your grille tell the builders' merchant exactly what you propose to do. A grille will ventilate the flue and deep a flow of dry air passing through it.

The other way out is to cap off the chimney at the top. This is a rather trickier operation, for it involves working up on the roof. Now it is all very well for the do-it-yourselfer to handle a ladder when he proposes to go no higher than the eaves, but lashing-up all the staging needed for working on a chimney is a different matter entirely.

If you can overcome this problem, then there is nothing to blocking off a chimney. You will see that the top of the chimney stack is covered with concrete, in which the chimney pots are embedded. This concrete is known as flaunching, and you remove it with a hammer and cold chisel. Next remove the chimney pots, by chipping round their bases with the hammer and cold chisel. Jam an old piece of slate into the top of the chimney, then fill up the opening to the top and renew the flaunching with a mixture of three parts of soft sand to one of cement, adding a proprietary waterproofer. You will have noticed how the flaunching sloped so that rainwater would run off it. You must shape your new flaunching in exactly the same way.

9

Simple furniture renovation

MIKE SMITH

The hard work in this part of the book is over and I would like to turn to something much less serious!

An odd phenomenon has manifested itself in those little roads off the High Street: junk furniture shops are springing up throughout the length and breadth of the land and people are flocking to them. By and large you cannot dignify the stuff that is sold there with the name of antiques. Often it does not even go back as far as the Victorian era (to be officially classified as antique, furniture must have been made before 1830). Anyway, the shortage of antique furniture has put such a premium on Victoriana that this, too, has become pricey and more difficult to find. So, a lot of what you see in the junk shops will be from the Edwardian era, some from the twenties, perhaps from the thirties, too. So help me, you even see being snapped up utility furniture made just after the war.

The reasons for the craze are obvious. In this mass-production era that tends to make everything and everybody look alike, the only way you can bring individuality to your home is to dash off to the street market and try to snap up a curio. Then there's the money factor. Junk furniture costs but a fraction of what you pay for new stuff. And that's not the whole of it. If you spend £100 on a brand new dining room suite today, then this time next year it is worth . . . what? £20? And three years later you will find it difficult to give away. But pay £4 for an Edwardian sideboard and a year later you can probably sell it for £5. It may well double in value over five years. And that is putting things at their worst.

For the eternal fascination of buying junk is the ever-present possibility that you might snap up a real treasure. Despite their all-knowing air, some owners of junk shops know very little about the subject. Even those that are really on the ball cannot be expert in everything. So you may, just may, pick up for a song something that is truly valuable.

But let us come down to earth and imagine that it is just a few ordinary items of everyday furniture you are buying second hand. What are you to do with them when you get them home? First take stock of what you have got. You may have bought a really nice piece of furniture made of most attractive wood, the only fault in which might be that it is slightly dirty. At specialist shops, you can buy cleaners, which can come in either paste or liquid form, specially to use on such furniture. They will give it a real spruce-up. You can follow up with a really good wax polish.

Sometimes, though, the furniture may be beautifully proportioned and made of really attractive timber, but the finish has deteriorated to the point where it really needs to be renewed. Perhaps even you might have to get rid of some really awful finish that a bungler has applied in the recent past. First you must get rid of the unsatisfactory finish. For this use an ordinary paint stripper, following closely the maker's instructions. The stripper is applied with a brush, and then you use a scraper to remove the varnish, polish etc. A broad flat scraper should be used on the large areas, and there is a whole series of shaped ones you can buy for dealing with the fiddly bits. If you do not have any of these scrapers, don't worry. You can use a ball of fine steel wool instead. Better wear old gloves when you do, though, for paint strippers are generally caustic and can burn the skin.

The old finish will probably not be entirely removed at your first attempt. Possibly you will need to have several tries, applying more stripper, then using your scraper or steel wool again, before you are satisfied. Finally, you must follow the maker's instructions about neutralising the stripper, because any traces of it left behind might well attack your new finish.

Now you must decide what this is going to be. A lot of old furniture looks most attractive left in its natural state. You can if you wish seal it—both matt and gloss seals are available. You can, too, polish it. True french polishing, in the traditional manner, is something that is beyond the scope of most amateurs, I feel, but many preparations are available to give a similar finish, and one that is truly hard wearing. A good wax polish used on its own gives a finish that appeals to many people.

Then, there is always paint. This is a finish that you would be well advised to use only on very recent furniture. Put paint on the older stuff, and you will be lowering its value. When you do paint furniture you have to be rather more careful than when you are dealing with, say, a skirting board or the outside of your house. For painted furniture becomes a specimen item that is really noticed, so you cannot just slap paint on and hope for the best. The procedure with specimen furniture should be to apply lots of thin coats, rather than one or two thick ones, rubbing down with a fine grade of glasspaper or steel wool in between. So after you have stripped it give your furniture a good sanding down. The sander you can fix to an electric drill is good for this, but use a finishing sander, not the disc type, whose action is much too severe for such work. Now apply a good coat of aluminium primer, pushing it well into the wood. When this has dried, fill up any holes and blemishes with a cellulose filler, sanding it down when it has set. Then apply an undercoat, following up with at least two top coats. For a really high-grade finish a third top coat would not come amiss.

One of the tell-tale signs that the work of painting a chest of drawers has been done by an amateur is the unsightly build-up of paint you get all round the top edge where it meets the sides. This arises because, as you apply your first brush strokes to the sides, paint oozes out and over on to the top. Similarly as your strokes on top approach the edges, paint will overflow down the sides. It does not need much paint to form a noticeable layer. The way to prevent this is to keep a dry brush handy and, when you have finished the top, use it to go all round the sides mopping up any surplus paint. Similarly, as you finish each side, run the dry brush along the adjacent parts of the top to wipe off any excess build-up.

A problem arises at the bottom of all pieces of furniture for, no matter how much paint finds its way to the old newspaper we put down to protect the floor, there will always be bare patches around the base of the furniture. The way to avoid these is to stand heavy carcase furniture—chests of drawers, wardrobes etc.—on battens to hold them well clear of the floor. Similarly, drive thin woodscrews into the legs of chairs and tables, to get the same effect.

Minor repairs

Of course, so far I have been assuming that the furniture you have bought is free from defect, and does not need any repairs. Such will not always be the case, by any means. Now, carrying out major repairs to furniture, and in particular antique restoration, is a job for the real craftsman. But minor repairs you can certainly do yourself. For a start, certain of the joints may have sprung apart, especially on the drawers. Gluing them together is easy, using modern woodworking adhesives. First chip off the old glue with a chisel or smooth it down with a rasp, then you can re-stick the joint again. One or more of the handles may be missing or damaged. You would be very lucky indeed to find a shop selling handles that would match, so you will probably have to remove all the old ones and fit a new set from scratch.

Lots of attractive handles are available today, so choose something suitable, both from the point of view of appearance, and the method of fitting. As for appearance, you want something that tones in with your furniture. Don't make the mistake of fitting ultra modern handles to Victoriana. One good rule is to avoid using a material that was not known at the time the furniture was built. For instance, wood and pottery are more suited to old furniture than plastic and chrome.

There are two normal methods by which modern handles are fitted. In one, a screw projects from the handle, and you fit it as you would any normal wood screw. That is, you drill a narrow gauge pilot hole, insert the point of the screw, and turn round the handle until it is fully home. Sometimes it is a bolt that protrudes from the handle. A hole of the same gauge as the bolt is bored, the bolt is cut to a length to suit the thickness of the door or drawer, the handle is pushed home and a nut placed on the bolt on the inside of the furniture.

Years ago it would not be a metal bolt that was used, but a round wooden peg that had been threaded. Now this wooden peg will have made rather a large hole, and whatever handle you choose must be shaped so that it covers this hole. But that is not the only aspect. The hole for the peg will be too big for the bolt of any modern handle, and of course you will not be able to drill a pilot hole for a screw there.

There are many ways out of this predicament. If the handle is big enough, you can drill new holes just slightly away from the the old one and let this be covered up by the handle. Actually, if you will be painting the furniture, you can stop up the hole with filler, and it will not be seen in the final result. Or you can jam lengths of dowelling, smeared with glue, into the old holes, and drill new holes in the dowels. This is particularly suitable for using a handle with a screw.

One other problem might be that there is worm present in the wood. Treat the affected areas with a proprietary woodworm killer, and then fill up the holes. One way of doing this is with a mixture of equal parts of beeswax and resin, which you heat up in a tin. When the two are thoroughly mixed, add a dye—this can be a wood stain, but even something such as a clothing dye would do—to bring it to the colour of the wood. Then spot the mixture into the holes, let it harden, and sand it down.

If this seems too much trouble, there is another dodge I would recommend. That is to go to a stationers and try to buy some sealing wax the same colour as the wood—yes, this is often possible. Heat the end of the stick of wax, and push this into the worm holes. Once again, sand down when the wax has hardened.

Stiff drawers

Another very common fault will be that the drawers do not operate smoothly. If it is that they are too stiff, try smoothing down with sandpaper the runners and the bottom of the drawer that comes in contact with them, then rub on soap or candle grease. If this does not work take a good look at the drawer as you pull it in and out slowly—it may be that you will see better if you pull out some or all of the other drawers in the chest. You might find it sticking somewhere, perhaps because it has been exposed to damp at some time, and parts of it have swelled up. A few strokes with a plane or Surform here and there should correct matters.

But the problem may be that the drawer sags when it is closed. This will be because the drawer runner is damaged in some way, or is missing altogether, or else there is something wrong with that part of the drawer that sits on the runner. Compare the drawer that has a defective action with those that work all right and you should soon see what is missing.

Dealing with the runner is easy. Prise off the defective one if it exists, causing as little damage as possible whilst you do this. Take a piece of wood of a size similar to the other runners—if you cannot buy timber the right size, get something slightly larger and plane it down to size—and fix it in place with glue and pins, taking care the pins are not so long that they will burst through the carcase. The runner has to be placed carefully. Its position must be true with the runner on the other side, otherwise you will not have effected a satisfactory cure.

Next deal with the drawer. Rip out any part that is defective. Once again you may have to buy timber slightly larger than needed, glue and pin it in place, then plane it flush and/or down to size.

Any strips of wood that are missing on the furniture may be dealt with in the same manner, although sometimes you can strip off broken pieces, and find the item just as attractive without them, particularly if you use your powered sander to smooth down the whole adjacent area.

It is worth while taking trouble with these finishing touches, and enjoyable, too. For one final attraction of buying up junk furniture and making it attractive is that you get the satisfaction that comes with a sense of achievement, with having created something; and yet are spared the problems that would undoubtedly have arisen if you had decided, say, that you were going to construct a built-in wardrobe from scratch.

10

House plants

GORDON COOPER

Halfway in the house and halfway outside, I suppose, and therefore a suitable close to this section on indoor improvements. I believe, in fact, that house plants are best looked at as an improvement to your home—like decorating, only more dramatic and exciting; like pictures on the walls, only with added versatility. I have in mind now an actual lounge of an acquaintance—ordinary and, if the truth were told, dull and conventional in appearance. This entire room is brought to life by a great hanging indoor ivy, trailing from a bowl high on the wall—magnificent.

I would like to emphasise the variety of opportunities available. Many of the plants we grow in the open garden can also be grown successfully indoors and, in addition, there are those which will only grow happily under cover. In such cases, the house is used as an extension of the greenhouse, as a means of protecting tender plants from other climates against the extremes of our weather. It is only by knowing something about the background of these plants that we can hope to put them in the best spot in the house and keep them growing well year after year.

Heat and light

In the greenhouse we can control temperature to ensure the correct conditions for the plants but this is not practical indoors, so we must choose the plants that will tolerate our room temperatures. Even these can vary widely according to the amount of heating available and the way in which it fluctuates during a 24-hour period. For example, a common cause of plant loss is putting plants on window sills where they get plenty of light and warmth during the day. But if they are left there when the curtains are drawn in the evening the drop in temperature can severely damage the plant. Remember also that few plants like to be in a draught—aspidistra, chlorophytum and cyssus antarctica are three that don't mind, but there are not many others. Gas fires are also a problem but the switch to natural or North Sea gas helps here, as the fumes are not nearly so harmful as those of traditional coal gas. An even temperature is the ideal as you can then choose the plants that thrive at that level. When temperatures fluctuate widely then you must select a plant that accepts the low temperature.

Like all other plants, house plants need adequate lighting to grow properly. This does not necessarily mean full sunlight and in fact many plants do not like it, preferring a good indirect light; some even prefer shade. Plants that get insufficient light become pale and spindly, and the new leaves put out get smaller and smaller. If this happens to your plant, move it closer to the window and it will soon recover if moved in time. Plants that are very close to a window sill lean towards it so they should be turned frequently to ensure balanced growth.

Humidity and watering

The amount of moisture in the air is important, particularly for those plants from tropical areas. You need a combination of warmth and moisture and you should not have one without the other. Many of the heating devices in our homes dry out the air so make sure not to place the plant in a warm, dry draught as this will dry it out very quickly.

One way to overcome the problem is to create a moist air "microclimate" around the plant by standing the pot on a shallow dish filled with pebbles. If you can keep ½ inch water in this tray, evaporation will keep the air around the plant moist. The plant troughs now available can be used in much the same way but in this case the pots are packed round with sphagnum moss which is kept moist to provide the moisture in the air. You will notice that in both these operations no mention has been made of watering as in neither case does any moisture get into the pot itself. Watering is another critical factor.

More house plants are killed by overwatering than any other

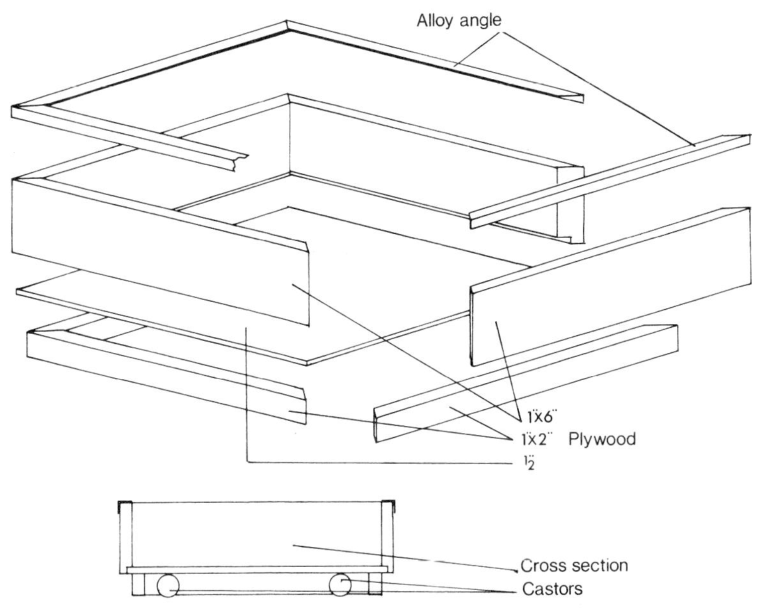

MOVABLE CONTAINER

This container is placed on castors so that you can move it around easily, and alter the position of your floral display without having to do any heavy lifting. It is intended primarily for use indoors—although it could be placed outside on the patio in fine, dry weather—therefore the plants will stand in pots, and thus the container itself needs no drainage holes.

The 6×1 inch sides are shown here as being joined with mitres, but if sawing these is beyond your carpentry abilities, you could use ordinary butt joints, although the effect would not be quite so neat. Mitred corners are also shown on the metal capping to the sides, but cutting these is a much simpler operation. The sides, too, are grooved to take the ½ inch thick plywood bottom, because this gives a more attractive effect. You could merely pin the bottom to the sides, however, if you do not have the necessary powered equipment for cutting out the groove. Castors are screwed to the bottom, and are hidden by a "skirt" of 2×1 inch timber. The castors should just protrude below this, and you might have to plane the timber down slightly to achieve this effect—it depends on what size castors you buy.

The completed movable container.

cause. There is no golden rule, as a large plant will need more moisture than a small plant and one that is pot bound, with the roots filling the pot, will need a lot of water to stay alive. The same plant will need more water in the summer when it is growing than it will in the winter when it is dormant. And remember, *this means the native winter of the plant, which may not be the same as ours.*

My advice on watering is this: choose your moment and then be bold and resolute. The best way to test moisture in the soil is with the fingers—if the top layer feels dry to the touch then it needs water. And, when you water, do it properly—no little dribbles to keep the plant going, as it were. The technique to employ is to immerse the whole pot in water until bubbles cease to rise from the soil. Since this is powerful treatment have some caution—namely, if in doubt, leave until tomorrow. Note also that soil in clay pots will dry out *immeasurably more quickly* than those in plastic pots, so be particularly attentive in such cases.

Feeding

As there is so little soil in a pot when compared with the soil the plant would utilise as a food source in the open garden, feeding is essential but it should not be overdone. After the end of October, when the plant is dormant, feeding will probably be unnecessary but once the plant starts to grow again in the spring then it is worth applying a liquid fertiliser strictly in accordance with the maker's instructions. Don't be tempted to add a drop more "for luck".

Potting and repotting

House plants are grown in compost which must be well drained. Plastic pots will satisfactorily drain themselves but the narrow base of a clay pot requires crocks for good drainage. There are two sorts of compost, both satisfactory—the John Innes range, which contains soil, and newer, soilless blends of peat and fertilisers (note: the latter are a devil to moisten once they are allowed to dry out).

Some plants will need repotting. Why is this? As plants grow the roots get bigger until the pot can no longer accommodate them. At this stage the plant in most cases shows signs of distress by growing slowly and drying out more quickly than usual. If you are in doubt turn the pot upside down and knock the edge against something firm; the soil will come out with the roots complete. You can then see just how tightly packed the roots are in the pot.

If the plant roots are congested then re-potting is called for. Take a pot a size larger, say from a three inch to a five inch. Cover the bottom with potting compost until, when you try the plant in the new pot, the original soil level is ¾ inch or so below the rim; then pack new compost into the space between the root ball and the side of the pot, leaving it at the same level in the new pot as it was in the old. The space at the top allows the water to be poured into it in adequate doses. This new soil must be firmed well down to hold the plant steady, and then watered. If your plant looks at all unhappy after re-potting then spray some tepid water over the foliage with a fine spray until it has settled in.

Choosing your plants

Well, where am I to start here? I don't know where in the house you intend to stand your purchases; I don't know how much growing room you have available; I don't know whether you want a bold display over a short period or a steady growth from year to year.

First, however, a general tip. The largest growers, Rochfords, have a labelling system that can be of use, so study your local supplier to see whether he has Rochford plants, which he most certainly will have. Look first at the colour of the label and choose according to your confidence: a pink label means "easy to look after", blue means "moderately difficult" and yellow means "delicate". When the choice is thus narrowed, look closer: the label will tell you the temperature tolerance, required situation and aspect and whether the plant is bought for its flowers or the foliage. It will not tell you whether the plant is an annual, bi-annual or perennial, nor how large it is likely to become, so these are the two questions you will still have to ask.

Why do house plants die

We have all asked this question—we seem to do everything but it is to little avail and the wretched things just droop and die on us. There are three main reasons.

Firstly, your plant may only be a single cycle plant; one season of flowering is all we can expect from this. I've frequently seen people feeding and watering in vain and they have been genuinely surprised when I've pointed out that the plant *wants* to die! Secondly, although the plant may be a perennial it may still need specialised treatment for prolongation into another year, i.e. it needs the facilities of a greenhouse. At the beginning of this chapter I suggested that the house is an extension of the greenhouse—don't forget that often it is an *inefficient* extension. Thirdly, there is overwatering or draughts.

Other than these, there is a fourth reason—sometimes plants just *do* die. That's gardening, my friend.

PART 2 JOBS OUTSIDE

11

Ladders and gutters

MIKE SMITH

Well, we've moved out of doors but, before we turn our attention to "the estate", there is one piece of equipment you generally use on the outside of the house and, apart from decorating, one particular, and important, job which can now be tackled by the average handyman. The equipment is the ladder and the job is guttering.

Now, a lot of householders are frightened of ladders. They find them such unwieldy brutes, almost with a will of their own, and quite untameable. But really a ladder is not something to be afraid of. Used properly and sensibly, it is a perfectly safe appliance. But, I must stress the importance of those words properly and sensibly.

First, though, where are you to get a ladder? The most obvious place is from a hire shop which will loan it out to you at quite a reasonable rate. However, if you are going to take care of your house properly, you will be using a ladder on quite a lot of occasions, and before you know where you are you will have paid out in hire fees more than the purchase price of a brand new one. So I would recommend that you buy one. Better still, get together with neighbours or friends, and share out the cost between you, each of you using it when needed.

Anyway, let us assume that you have bought your ladder and there it is, lying flat on the ground, waiting to be used. The first problem is: how do you raise it to the upright position? Well, the man not used to handling ladders needs a helper. Get him (or her, for that matter) to stand at one end of the ladder with his foot firmly on the last rung, whilst you stand at the other end.

Now bend your legs and crouch down, taking hold of your end of the ladder. Straighten your legs, raising yourself up, and you will bring the ladder up to waist height. It is important to use the strength of your legs, rather than your back, to avoid a back injury. Now raise the ladder above your head, and start to walk towards your helper, raising the ladder all the time as you go. Your helper should be keeping the ladder firmly anchored to the ground, otherwise, as you reach about half way, your arms would act as the fulcrum of a see-saw and the ladder would go swinging about and career out of control. Eventually, you will reach the fully vertical position, and you can take over from your helper.

If you cannot get a helper, you can often obtain the same effect by jamming the ladder up against the bottom of a wall, but this method is more risky.

Now comes the job of moving an erect ladder. You stand hard up against one side of it, with, for a right handed person, your right shoulder jammed up against it. Raise your left arm and grab the highest rung you can, on the same side of the ladder as yourself. Curl your right arm round the back of the ladder, and grab a rung low down. Thus you have gripped the ladder in a sort of wrestler's lock and you can carry it around.

If your ladder is an extension one, then you may find it more convenient to raise it and carry it around in two separate halves, joining them up when they are in position leaned up against a wall. It is important to place the ladder at the correct angle to the wall—which is one foot out for every four foot of rise. In other words, if the top of your ladder touches a point 12 foot high on the wall the other end should be 3 foot away from the base of the wall.

For the amateur, the easiest kind of ladder to handle is the one that is extended with ropes; otherwise you have to push the top half up with your hands. That is all right for the first few feet, but the occasion may arise when you actually have to be standing halfway up the bottom part of the ladder to push the top half further up still and that can be tricky. In fact, in such an instance, you would be better off extending your ladder before you raise it and while it is still flat on the ground.

Making the ladder secure

Now that the ladder is up, your main concern should be to see

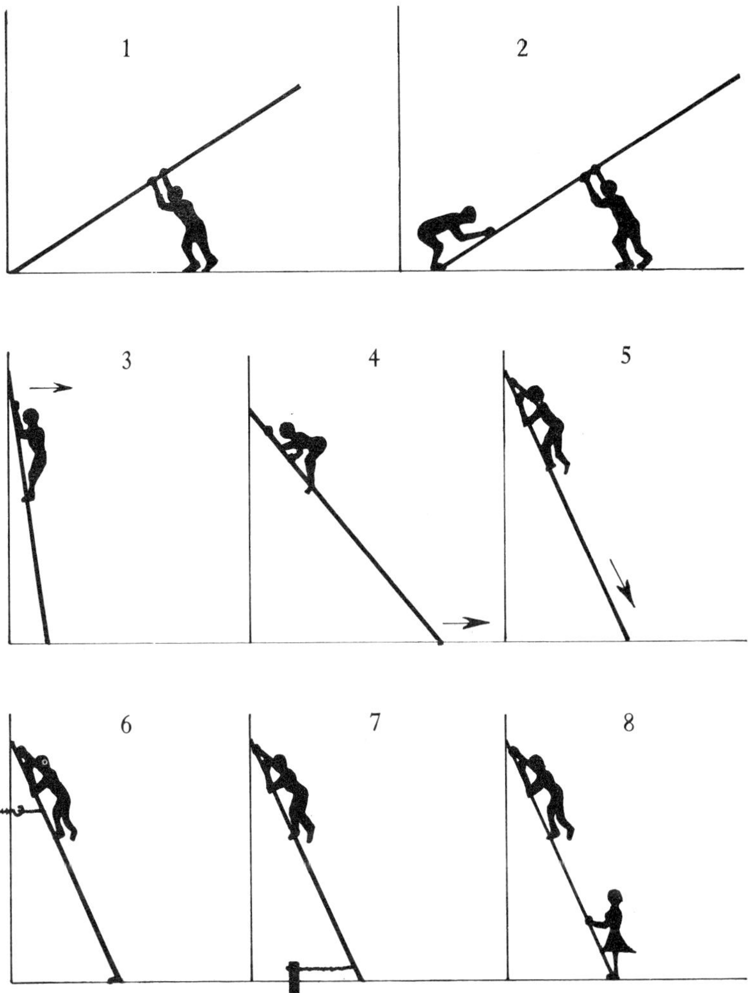

HOW TO USE A LADDER SAFELY

1. When raising it, jam the foot of it against a wall.
2. . . . or get a helper to anchor it securely against the ground.
3. When erected a ladder should be 1 foot out from the wall for every 4 feet of height. Too near, and the top might fall away . . .
4. . . . too far and the bottom might start to slide.
5. Walk up the ladder properly or you might fall down.
6. The top of the ladder can be lashed to screw eyes.
7. The bottom can be tied to a stake driven into the ground.
8. . . . or you can get a helper to steady it for you.

that it doesn't slip down, bringing yourself with it. There are several things you can do to ensure this. First, look at the ground it will stand on. Is it soft, so that the ladder tends to sink into it? Then you want to make sure that both legs sink in to an equal depth, for a slight variation at ground level will mean an enormous one at the top, where you will be standing. If you are in any doubt, lay a flat board on the ground and place the ladder on that.

Now you want to stop the ladder from slipping away from the wall. If you are on garden soil, this is easy. You drive a stake into the ground and lash the ladder to this. If you have to place the ladder on a garden path, then perhaps there is a flower bed sufficiently close at hand into which you can drive stakes. But on a large expanse of concrete—a patio or a garage drive—you will have to adopt other methods. A piece of old sacking placed under the ladder will increase friction and minimise the chance of the ladder sliding over smooth concrete. There might be something you can tie a ladder to. One idea is to pass rope through the letter box and tie it round the newel post of the staircase. Of course, you could always get your wife to stand at the bottom of the ladder, and hold it. Failing all else, you can use masonry pins, to nail a batten to the concrete to wedge the ladder in place. Don't, however, lash your ladder to a drain pipe. It probably isn't fixed securely enough.

Now for safety at the top. If you feel at all precarious up there, lash the ladder to screw eyes driven into the fascia. Once you have inserted the screw eyes you can leave them there permanently for next time you want to use the ladder—they will not be noticeable from the ground. When you are working near a window, open those that are hinged and you will then be able to tie the ladder to the frame.

Another problem at the top end of a ladder can be that the very spot where you need to rest your ladder in order to reach whatever part of the house you want to deal with is right in the middle of a window pane. If you do that, of course, the minute you rest your weight on the ladder there is more than a risk that you will crack the glass. The way to avoid this is to lash a length of timber—you will find something like 3 × 1 inch to be a suitable size—across the top of the ladder. This timber will rest either on parts of the window frame, or even on the wall each side of it, so that the ladder is held clear of the glass.

Don't carry anything in your hands as you climb up a ladder. You ought to wear an apron or overalls with lots of pockets into which you can put everything you will need. If there are too many tools for you to do this, put them in a bucket to which a long length of rope is tied, and haul this up after you. An opened can of paint is a problem. You should have a container with a handle on it so that once again you can haul this up with rope.

It is important, too, to wear the right sort of shoes. Many amateurs wear such things as old tennis shoes because they think the rubber soles will give them a better grip on the rungs. But your feet will tire very quickly if you are standing on a ladder for a long time wearing thin soled shoes, so you would really be better off with the stoutest boots you can find. Before you start to climb check that the boot laces are securely tied. You don't want to risk tripping up on them on top of a ladder. It's not a bad idea to wear cycle clips on your trousers, or at least tuck the pants in your socks, for you might trip up over the ends of these, too.

Finally, try to pick a day that isn't very windy for working up a ladder, at least until you are more accustomed to handling one.

Repairs to guttering

Now for the defective guttering. If you ever have reason to suspect that anything is wrong with your rainwater goods—as they are known in the trade—you should take steps to remedy the fault immediately. For it is important that these perform efficiently their task of collecting water from the roof and taking it speedily out of harm's way down to the drains. For once they cease to do this, there is a risk that water will overflow and start to rot exterior woodwork, and perhaps make the house walls damp. This damp can penetrate into the inside of the house—especially in old homes that are not built of cavity walls—harming decorations, and eventually causing the plaster to come away from the walls.

One of the most common guttering faults is that they become blocked with an accumulation of dirt and leaves. The remedy here is simple. You take a small trowel up to the guttering and scoop out the rubble. Anyone living in a heavily wooded area with lots of trees overhanging his property should inspect the gutters every autumn, once the leaf-fall has finished, to see if there is any need to carry out clearance work. If trouble occurs regularly, it is

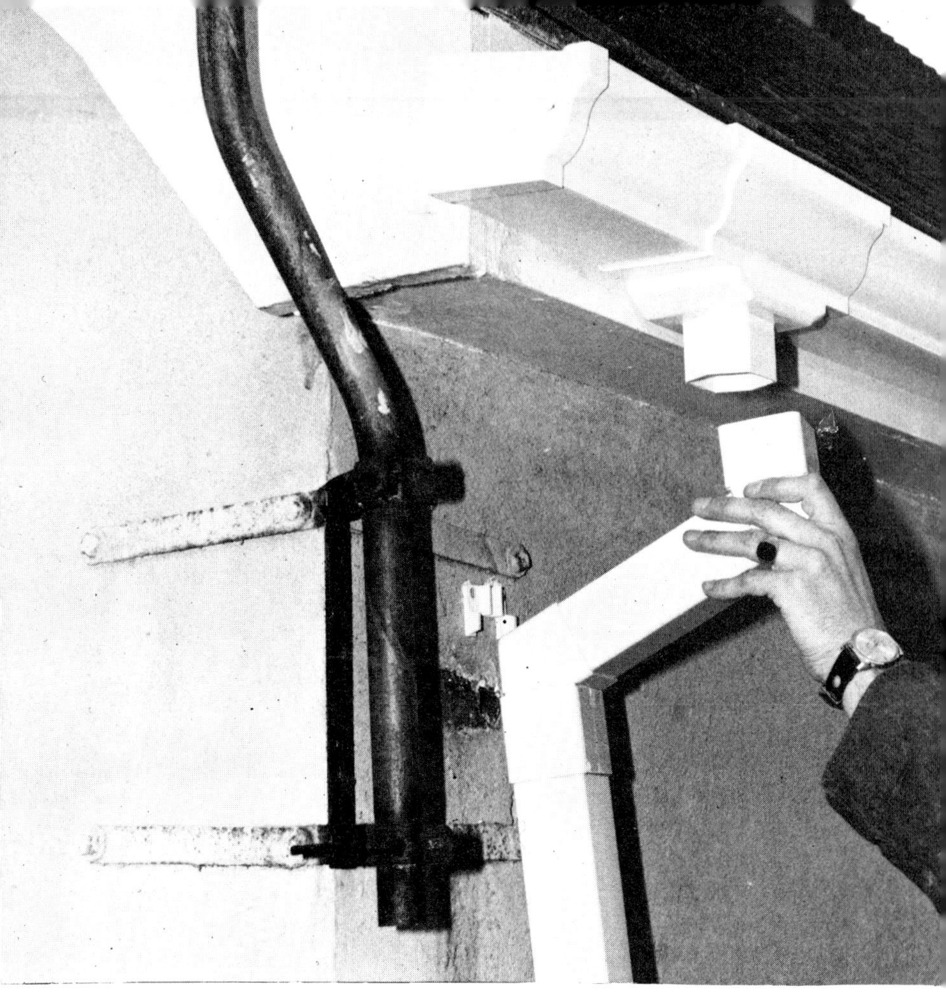

Fixing plastic rainwater goods; note the attractive styling.

probably worth while fixing a guard of some sort. You can buy these, or devise one yourself from wire netting—the plastic ki ıd is eminently suitable. You merely bend a suitable length of this netting and jam it in the guttering, where it will spring back to hold itself securely in place.

The blockage may be not in the guttering, but in a downspout. The joins between the various sections of these should never be sealed so that water pouring out of them after a heavy downfall will show you in which section the blockage occurs. How to cure a blockage? You will have to climb up your ladder and push a long length of stick or cane down the pipework.

Joints between the sections of guttering should be sealed, and sometimes the seal breaks down. You will then have to remove the bolt holding the two sections together, scrape off the old sealant and apply new. If you are lucky the bolt will simply unscrew but in many cases you will have to saw through it with a hacksaw.

A guttering bracket can corrode over the years and rob the gutter of its support at this point. As a result, the gutter will sag, allowing water to pour over the sides. You may be able to prop it up by inserting bits of metal between the gutter and bracket but in most cases the bracket will have to be removed and replaced with a new one. In ideal circumstances, the screws holding the bracket should be capable of being withdrawn in the normal way with a screwdriver but generally everything will be so rusted up that you will have to wrench the bracket away. Erecting the new bracket should not, of course, present any problems.

Replacing guttering

Because of rust, holes may have developed in sections of the system and these can be repaired with a fibreglass kit. But eventually, the whole lot may have rotted away so much that the only thing to do is scrap it and put up something new in its place.

Your first job is to choose and buy the replacements, for you must have these ready to put up as soon as you have taken the old lot down. Otherwise you might get a prolonged spell of heavy rain and water would come cascading down the walls of your house, soaking the whole fabric and anybody who happens to be in the way.

I would strongly urge that you choose a plastic replacement. Plastic rainwater goods have many advantages over the cast iron stuff, even though they cost more. For instance, they will not rust or rot, and you never need to paint them, although they will take gloss paint if you want them to match the colour scheme of the rest of the house. Furthermore since the insides are much smoother, there is less chance of a blockage developing. But the overwhelming advantage of plastic for the do-it-yourselfer is that it is much lighter and so you will find it much easier and safer to handle up at roof level.

Traditionally, downspouts have always been round and guttering half round, but some attractive alternatives are available in plastic—for instance square section stuff. Go and study the catalogues—I think you will be surprised by what you can buy. Having chosen, you must now plan a system to suit your house. Basically, this means going round the outside with a rule and the maker's catalogue and plotting something very similar to what you already have. As you will see, there is a very wide range of fittings, in the form of joints, angles, hoppers etc. You will soon be able to work out exactly what you need.

Once you have ordered the stuff and it has been delivered, you can start to dismantle the old system. The guttering itself should be no problem. If it is old enough to be in very bad condition, then it is sure to be made of cast iron. This merely sits on the brackets screwed to the fascia—it relies on its weight to hold it in place—although various sections of it may be bolted together. You would probably be well advised to separate it into sections and to do so you will probably have to saw through the bolts with a hacksaw. Take care how you get the guttering down to the ground. Remember you are handling heavy unwieldy objects at the top of a ladder and you will need to watch your step. In fact, you will very soon appreciate the wisdom of buying plastic replacements. You could, of course, just throw the stuff to the ground; be sure, if you do that no one is down there! Better to tie rope to the guttering, and lower it down gently.

Next you must get rid of the brackets that held the gutters. In theory this should be very easy. You ought merely to have to withdraw a few screws. But if the gutters are in such a state that they need complete renewal, then you can bet the bracket screws are so rusted up that no screwdriver is going to budge them. Once again, you will probably have to wrench everything off, using a small crowbar, a strong old screwdriver, or a claw hammer.

You will probably have to get out a hacksaw to free the bolts holding the various hoppers and downspouts etc. I would advise you to take great caution here in case anything goes clattering down to the ground once a bolt or retaining clip is prised free. In particular, make sure your wife keeps your children well out of harm's way.

Plastic guttering is very easy for the amateur to install. The gutter is held to the fascia on a series of brackets to which it will be clipped. It is important to make sure that the gutter slopes towards its downspout—that it has, as tradesmen say, a fall.

A fall would usually be described by some expression such as 1 inch in 10 foot. A good way to ensure that you get the correct fall as specified by the manufacturer, is to drive a nail into one end of the fascia board. Now insert another nail at the opposite end, but putting it on a lower level than the first one, according to the distance it is away. Then run a string between the two nails. This will be a guide line to help you screw the brackets in place at the correct height.

The downspouts need to be fixed truly vertically and the way to ensure that is to nail a length of rope in the correct position on the fascia and attack a weight to the end of it. Brackets and joining sections will be used to attach the downspouts to the wall. They will be fixed by screws driven into wall plugs.

If it seems as though I am being a little vague about exactly how the fixing is carried out, then that is deliberate. For each system has its own little quirks and there would be no point in describing one of them here, for it might not be the system you would buy. However full instruction sheets are available from the makers, and they show in a clear graphic form exactly what needs to be done. I do assure you that the installation is well within the competence of the amateur builder. Anyone who can drive screws into wood and fix plugs to a wall can fix rainwater goods.

12

Making a patio

MIKE SMITH

Our next job still lies near to the house and can almost be regarded as an extension—an extra room going begging outside every back door or french windows. A patio can act as a sitting-out area, play space for children, a spot where you can have breakfast and other meals, in short a general outdoor room. Now, I know it can be used only in warm, dry weather, and it is easy to be cynical about how little of that we get in Britain. Yet, you know, we do get more sunnier days than we like to admit—certainly enough, I feel, to justify building a patio.

In fact, building a patio can be as simple as laying a concrete raft in your garden, as described in the next chapter. I think, however, that most people would want something a little more decorative than that.

So first . . . where is your patio going to be? The obvious place is just outside your french windows, if you have them. The more accessible your patio, the better for serving meals and snacks, and for keeping an eye on the children. But that is not the only consideration. Suppose the back of your house faces north. Build your patio there and you would always be sitting out in the shade—not exactly ideal for sunbathing. In cases like that you can break entirely with tradition and put your patio right at the top of the garden—anywhere so long as it is in the sun. Yes, I know you will be more exposed up there both to cooling winds and prying neighbours. But you can always create shelter and privacy by a hedge or a wall—perhaps one made of the now very popular screen blocks.

There is also another point. A patio adjoining to the house should slope away from it slightly, so that rainwater runs off and does not lodge against the house. It should also be at least 6 inch below the level of the dampproof course, if you have one.

You can easily spot a dampproof course. It's where a horizontal bed of mortar looks twice as thick as all the others. Now it may be that the contours of your garden—as, for instance, if it slopes towards your house—will prevent your fulfilling these conditions without a lot of excavation that you would rather not tackle. So that's yet another reason for building your patio right away from the house. Even at the top of the garden, your patio needs to slope slightly (in whatever direction is most convenient) so that rain-water will not lodge in the middle of it.

How to use paving slabs

Now . . . what is the surface of your patio to be? The obvious choice is paving slabs. You can buy slabs in various natural stones from a garden supplier, or perhaps approach a local council or demolition contractor when old houses are being pulled down.

You can also buy concrete slabs in a wide variety of sizes and colours. Firms selling them often suggest patterns in which slabs of different sizes can be grouped together to form an interesting effect. You can, too, make concrete slabs yourself. You get a firm level site, bash the earth down hard, and set up formwork of 2×1 inch timber, held in place by pegs. Sprinkle a $\frac{1}{2}$ inch layer of damp sand over the whole area inside the formwork and make sure that the sand is level. Pour a concrete mix of 1 part of cement to 3 of sand (see p. 107) into the framework, and smooth the surface. When the concrete has stiffened, but before it sets hard, cut it into slabs of the size you want, using a pointing trowel.

After four of five days, the slabs can be lifted with a spade and stacked until they are needed. Until then, keep them damp, and protected from sun and wind.

You have to take a certain amount of care with the cutting. For instance, make sure you cut right through the concrete. Be certain, too, that the slabs you create will be square and of an accurate size, otherwise you will have difficulties when you come to lay them. Measure carefully, lay a true, straight board across the formwork and use it as a straightedge, to hold your trowel against as you cut.

How big should the slabs be? That is entirely up to you. On a big area, a lot of small slabs will look fussy, but small slabs can make tiny patios look bigger. Suitable sizes are 12, 18 and 24 inch square, or you can have rectangular slabs 2 × 1 foot, or 18 × 9 inch. Remember, though, that the bigger the slabs the heavier they will be to carry.

There are two ways of laying the slabs—and they are known as the dry and the wet methods. With both, you first of all excavate as necessary, and firmly compact the base, using either an iron rammer, or a good trampling with your heels. Then for the dry method you mix a compost of equal parts of sand, peat, and finely mixed soil. Bed the slabs in the compost and press them down evenly with a wooden rammer. Finally, brush a mixture of the compost into the joins between the slabs. These joins, incidentally, should be 1 inch wide, and you can if you wish plant ground cover plants such as thyme and saxifrage in them.

For the wet method, you spread a 2 inch layer of mortar (1 part cement to four of soft sand, with just enough water added to make it stiff and moist, but not runny) on a 4 inch base of clinker or hardcore. The slabs are set in this, a ½ inch gap is left between them, and this is pointed with a mortar of 1 part of cement to 2 of soft sand.

Which of these methods is preferable? It depends. Obviously the dry one is quicker and less tiring but a patio laid by the wet method is stronger and will stand up to heavier traffic. Whichever you use, set out the boundary of the patio with string and pegs, to show you exactly the area you need to excavate and to indicate the line to which the slabs should be laid. Make frequent checks as you work, with a level placed on a long board, to ensure that you are laying everything level—or should one say slightly sloping. Do not cover the whole area with compost or mortar at one go, but work on two square yards or so at a time. Otherwise you would be walking on newly laid compost and so disturbing it, or having to stand on wet mortar.

You can add interest to a large area of slabs by missing one out here and there, either at random, or in a formal pattern, and planting flowers or shrubs in the space, or filling it with cobble stones. On a dry base, you merely bed the stones in with a wooden rammer, then "grout" areas between them with a mix of the base compost. If you have used the wet method, set the cobbles in a mix of 1 of cement to 2 of soft sand.

Crazy paving

Slabs create a formal effect that is suited to a modern building, or a town garden. If you want a country cottage atmosphere, you might prefer crazy paving instead. Once more, you can choose either a wet or dry method, and you lay the stones in exactly the same way as slabs. Begin at the edges with larger stones, and work inwards, making frequent checks that everything is to the correct slope.

Just as it is possible to make your own concrete slabs with concrete, so, too, can you make crazy paving. However, this time you do not, obviously, have to worry about cutting the "stones" accurately and squarely to shape. It does, however, pay you to take care to create an attractive pattern. When you take the "stones" up, lay them in exactly the same relationship to each other to avoid having the "jig-saw puzzle" problem that is usual when setting-out crazy paving.

A brick patio

Another suitable surfacing for patios is brick, and this is a material that sets off handsomely certain styles of house. It is true that it can be an expensive and fiddly method of creating a patio but, should you be able to get hold of bricks from a demolition site or suchlike, then it becomes an attractive proposition.

Bricks for a patio are placed edge on with ½ inch gaps between and with the sides showing, as in a wall. Once again there are two principal methods of laying them. With the first, you prepare a hardcore base, then bed the bricks in a 2 inch layer of soft sand, except for the edging bricks, which should go in a mix of 1 part of cement to 3 of sand to hold them firmly in place. Dry sand should then be brushed over the surface to fill in the gaps between the bricks.

The second method involves spreading a dry mix of 1 part of cement to 4 of sand over a clinker or hardcore base, and bedding the bricks in this. Once again ½ inch gaps should be left and these are filled by brushing the mix into them. Once the surface is complete, spray the whole area with water, then let it dry off and the resulting cement set before using the patio.

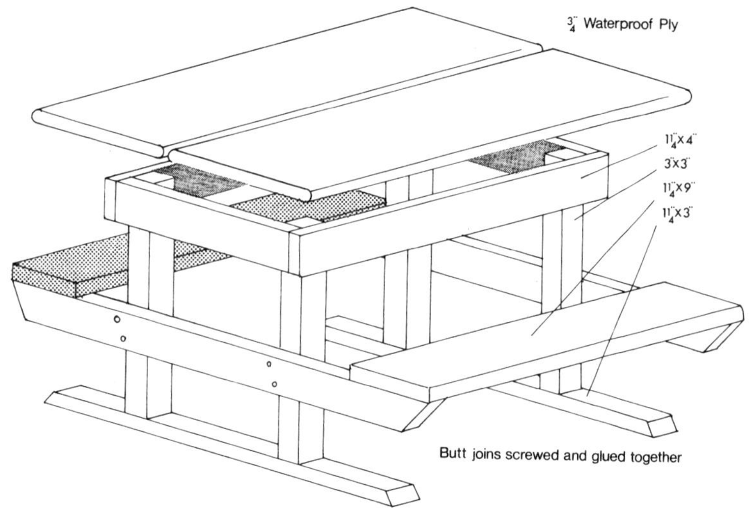

A seat for garden or terrace.

Asphalt

Asphalt is also another surface used for patios but only the cold stuff is suitable for amateur use and not the hot asphalt that road repairers use. Cold asphalt is supplied in bags in proprietary form, and comes with full instructions. Decorative stones chips are sprinkled into it, and the whole surface finally smoothed over with a roller. This material is eminently suitable for renovating an old patio that is no longer in very good condition—particularly a concrete raft that has cracked and chipped.

Having created your patio, you might now feel that a path leading from it to the other parts of your garden would be a nice idea. You make this in pretty much the same way, using paving stones, crazy paving, bricks or concrete, except that since it is smaller and would probably not receive quite the same traffic, you can afford to skimp a little on the foundations.

Patio furniture

Having built your patio, you will need to furnish it if you are to enjoy it to the full. Deck chairs and tubular aluminium chairs and sun beds are obvious good buys. But my sketch shows something you can make to be left permanently out of doors. It's a family-size table, incorporating its own seating, on which you can take breakfast or lunch in sunny weather, perhaps even meals late at night during a real heat wave.

I think you will see at a glance how it is made. It has all been designed for easy construction—butt joints glued and screwed together are used throughout. The timber should all be fairly easy to buy from a good woodyard, although you do not have to follow my sizes exactly. The thing you may have difficult with is $\frac{3}{4}$ inch thick plywood. You could get by with $\frac{1}{2}$ inch thick ply, although I feel it would look too thin for the rest of the construction. I would be inclined to buy $\frac{1}{2}$ inch and $\frac{3}{8}$ inch ply, and glue them together.

Since the table is to stand out of doors in all weather, use non-rusting screws and waterproof glue throughout. The finished item will also need protection. You can either paint it, or treat it with a proprietary preservative, suitable for use out of doors.

13

Using concrete

MIKE SMITH

As the previous chapter on patios makes clear, you can't progress far in jobs out of doors before you need concrete. If you have never worked with it, then I would strongly urge you to try. Concrete is most useful and versatile. You can use it for anything from repairing the fabric of your house to building garden ornaments and statuary. But your first experiences with it are likely to be much more humdrum than that, and you will probably be doing things like making a garden path, a base for a shed or greenhouse, or a patio.

Concreting, at least on a do-it-yourself scale, requires few tools and not much skill. What tools do you need? A long-handled spade or shovel, a watering can, household bucket, trowel, steel or wooden float, and timber to make the mould (the formwork as builders call it) for whatever it is you are building. And that's about all. As for the skill, I hope you will have that after reading this chapter. There is, of course, considerable effort involved, and if it is your first try, you must expect a lot of aching muscles when you have finished. However, providing you are a fit person and suffer from no back or muscle trouble, you should be all right.

First of all, though, what is concrete? The study of it is a vast technology itself but, as far as the DIY man is concerned, you can say that four ingredients go to make up concrete. They are cement, sand, aggregate and water. The first three of these are mixed in varying proportions according to the job for which the concrete is to be used—you get a sort of recipe—then water is added. In addition, certain jobs may call for the addition of a waterproofer (this is most likely to be when you are building a pool) and you can add colouring agents. I would advise you, however, to gain a little experience before you try to colour concrete.

Many specialist types of cement are sold, but the ordinary Portland cement will suit you for most occasions. There are, however, two kinds of sand—sharp and soft. Sharp sand is the coarser of the two, and contains lots of very fine pebbles. Because of this it is sometimes known as fine aggregate. Sharp sand is the type you use on concrete. Soft sand is more refined, usually golden in colour. It is used for mortars. The aggregate is usually gravel, sometimes called shingle, although other materials can be used. It varies in size from $\frac{3}{16}$ to $\frac{3}{4}$ inch, and the larger it is the coarser the finished product. For all general work around the garden, $\frac{3}{8}$ inch gravel is satisfactory.

So far I have described all the various materials separately, but it is possible to buy some of them ready mixed. For instance, you can buy an "all-in" ballast with sand and gravel ready mixed, although this is not suitable for finer work. You can buy ready-mixed mortars, too, and in very tiny quantities—very handy for those small repair jobs.

Large concreting jobs

Most of the concreting instructions for do-it-yourselfers describe how to mix by hand, and this is a perfectly satisfactory way, as far as the final result is concerned. It is the method the professionals use when they are working on small jobs. But even they would baulk at hand-mixing the quantities needed for some of the jobs a DIY man would tackle—for a garage base and drive, for instance. At the very least they would bring along a cement mixer. Can you do the same? Of course. Lots of firms will hire these out—look at the advertisements in your local paper, or the Yellow Pages of your telephone directory.

There is a way to cut down on the hard work even further, and that is to buy ready-mixed concrete. Yes, those huge lorries that service the building sites are willing to come and deliver to you. They will insist on a minimum load, however, the usual stipulation being from 3 cubic foot upwards—an amount you might easily use on the example I have already cited, a garage and drive.

There are many advantages to using a ready-mixed concrete,

apart from the fact of cutting down on hard work. Not the least of these is that you can be sure that the concrete will be of pure materials and mixed to the right consistency.

The big snag, however, is that you have only about one hour in which to use it all up, for after that it will have set. If there is access for the lorry to dump the concrete exactly where you want it, then fine. But otherwise you are going to need a lot of helpers at the ready, plus wheelbarrows and spades.

Concreting by hand

However, for the rest of the chapter I will assume that, since you are a beginner, you will be dealing with small quantities and thus working by hand.

A mix is usually expressed with the cement first, then the sand and finally the aggregate. So if you read in your "recipe" that you need a 1:2:4 mix, you will know it means 1 part of cement to 2 of sand to 4 of aggregate. And it is, of course, parts by volume, not weight, that are meant. Three very handy mixes for use around the house and garden are: 1:2½:4 for garden rollers and thick walls; 1:2:3 for paths, pools, steps, garden frames, pots, edging, and thin sections; 1:2:0 for artificial rocks, formal or crazy paving less than 2 inch thick, mortar.

Before you mix, though, you must obviously prepare your site. If you want the area of concrete you are to lay (the builder, incidentally, calls it a raft or slab) to finish flush with the surrounding soil you will have to excavate. If you want it to be proud of the soil then you must build a framework of 1 inch thick boards, held in place by pegs driven into the ground. In fact, it is probably still as well to construct a framework even when you have excavated. Your slab should not be laid perfectly level but should slope—away from a house or outbuilding, for instance—so that rainwater will drain from it. Your framework should therefore be fixed to a slope—use a spirit level to check this. If the concrete base for a shed etc. is to extend beyond the perimeter of the building then it should slope on all edges to carry the rainwater away. If rainwater were allowed to lodge near the constructional timbers of your outbuilding, then it might cause them to rot, no matter how much protection you gave in the way of paint or preservative.

For such a base, or a patio, a depth of concrete 3 inch would be suitable, and for a garden path where traffic will be light, 2 inch would be adequate. The concrete has, however, to be laid on a firm base, otherwise it would crack. So make sure that the soil on which the concrete will be laid is hard packed. Fill in any soft spot or hollows with what the builder calls hardcore—broken bricks and similar rubble. Make sure that the whole area is well compacted—a heavy garden roller is an ideal appliance for doing this, otherwise you will have to bash it with your spade.

A much stronger construction would be needed to form, say, a garage, or a drive, or a base for a home extension. Then, you would need a 3 inch layer of well-rammed hardcore, topped with concrete at least 4 inch thick.

Where, incidentally, do you buy the various materials? From a builder's merchant. Do not be tempted to get any of it wild—by, for example, picking up pebbles from a beach, or sand from a river bank. Such materials will contain impurities, which will harm the final work. Despite its association with the rough conditions of the building site, concrete needs to be made carefully from well measured, clean and pure materials.

Once your materials have been delivered, you must protect them from damp and frost. The cement particularly needs to be kept dry. Try to store it in a shed or similar outbuilding, on a timber floor. The sand and hardcore can be kept out of doors but throw a cover over them. Never use wet or frost-covered materials for making concrete. No water should touch them until they have all been thoroughly mixed.

How to mix

An ordinary household bucket is as good as anything for measuring the ingredients. First measure out the amount of aggregate needed and dump it on a clean hard surface—dry concrete already laid and from which you have brushed all dust and dirt, or a sheet of blockboard will do. Never mix concrete on garden soil. Now dump the required sand on to the aggregate, and mix them together. You do this by sticking your spade in the bottom of the pile and turning the whole lot over. If you can get a helper to work from one side whilst you mix at the side opposite him, so much the better. If you can't, dump your ingredients at one end of the board and as you turn you will see them gradually move to the other. You then start at this end and bring the pile back again. When the sand and aggregate are mixed, add the cement and turn the ingredients over again. You will know that everything is well enough mixed when you see that it is all a uniform colour.

Now you are ready to add water. Dig out a hole in the centre of your mix, pour into it water from your watering can used without rose and once more turn the ingredients over. If the mix is then too dry you can always sprinkle more water from the can with the rose on. The mistake that most amateurs make when adding water, however, is that they slop on far too much. Although a recipe for specialist work may give different instructions, by and large the general rule is that you should add just enough water to bind the mix together, and no more. There is a simple test you can carry out to make sure whether your mix is too sloppy. Fill your bucket with the concrete, then turn it upside down and, like a child on the beach, make a "pie" of it. The concrete will then slump. If that slump is within 2 inch of the height of the bucket, then the consistency is correct. I am not suggesting that you carry out such a slump test every time you mix concrete but only during your first few tries. Eventually, you will be sufficiently experienced to judge when the mix is just right. But you must take some trouble to ensure that it is. Concrete that is mixed too wet is very weak stuff that will crack and disintegrate easily, and become dusty, too.

Laying the concrete

Now you are ready to lay the concrete. It is important, however, that it should not go on a base that is too dry, otherwise the moisture will be sucked out of it and it will dry out too quickly. And that, too, will result in a weak raft. So in hot, dry weather damp down the base first by sprinkling water from your can. Once again, however, you must not overdo things. If the base is soil, you want to be sure it is firm yet damp earth you'll be putting your concrete on, not mud. Similarly, should you be laying your concrete on a base of hardcore, pour on just enough water to be soaked up into the broken bricks and not so much that there will be pools lying underneath.

Shovel your mixed concrete on to the site, and spread it out. The mix needs to be well tamped down to ensure that no air bubbles are trapped in it, for these could burst, causing cracks. Especially do you need to ensure that it fills up the cavities in the

1.
Tamping down a concrete path.

2.
Brushing down gives a textured effect.

3.
Erecting formwork for a path.

4.
A tougher tamping board is needed for bigger jobs.

5.
Checking that the path formwork slopes.

hardcore. You can use a spade or a board for the tamping, paying particular attention to the edges. Finally, place a board across your work, its ends resting on the framework on each side, and get someone to help you tamp it down. Begin with an up-and-down chopping movement of the board, then slide it along to get rid of surplus concrete. This method produces a rippled non-slip surface that is good for drives and paths. If you want a smooth surface, you must trowel over it with a steel or wooden float. If you want a textured effect, brush over it with a good, stiff yard brush.

The longer the concrete can be left to dry off, the better. So once it starts to harden cover it with wet sacks or damp sand to protect it from the drying action of sun and wind. After a day or so, you can even hose it down or sprinkle water from a watering can on it. In fact, it really is better to delay your concreting if a heatwave comes along just as you planned to start work, but this is not always possible. Still, providing you keep the work moist, it should be all right.

But you should never in any circumstances lay concrete if frost is forecast. Should frost come unexpectedly after you have laid concrete, then cover it with a protective coating of straw or a thick layer of newspapers.

In warm weather, concrete will harden enough to take light loads in about four days, although it might be safer to wait ten days when the weather is cool. If it is a drive you have laid, then you can take your car across it after ten days or so but, should all the hard work have convinced you that for your next spell of concreting you are going to order ready mixed stuff, then wait three weeks—for it will take that long before you dare let a lorry drive over it.

The greenhouse base

It might not always be a raft of concrete you are constructing. You might, for instance, want to build foundations as for when you are erecting a greenhouse.

Although a greenhouse is not a very cumbersome structure, there is enough weight there to cause it eventually to sink into even the firmest ground. Therefore a foundation of some sort is advisable in most cases, and essential on very soft ground.

Mark out the perimeter of the greenhouse on the site you have

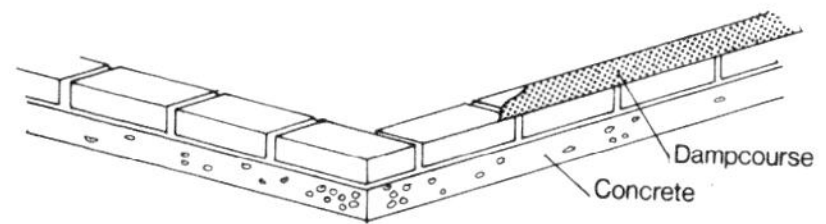

A suitable base for a greenhouse.

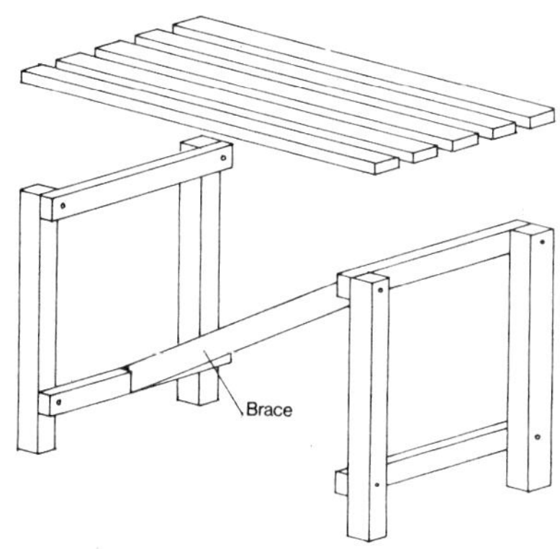

GREENHOUSE STAGING

The legs of this greenhouse staging are of 2 inch square timber, but all the rest is 2×1 inch. The horizontal members are first screwed to the legs, and then the top slats are nailed in place. The only complication about the construction is that the brace is fixed to the horizontal members by means of what is known as a bird's mouth joint. This can be quite tricky to cut and you could, if you wish, use instead a brace screwed to the inside of the two front legs, with another fixed in a similar fashion to the back legs.

chosen and dig a trench, deep enough to take 3 inch of concrete and slightly more than one course of brickwork. Compact the bottom of the trench, then drive in two or three pegs according to the size of your trench. Leave the pegs projecting by 3 inch. Lay a board across the pegs and check that they are level by placing a spirit level on the board. Adjust the pegs if necessary.

Now you can lay the concrete. Place the board across the pegs to make sure not only that the foundations are level but also that the concrete is to the correct depth. Let the concrete set hard and lay two courses of brickwork on it. Thus part of one course of brickwork will be projecting from the ground. Fill in the trench with the earth you have dug out up to the level of the surrounding soil, and your greenhouse can now sit on the brickwork.

What about an actual floor for the greenhouse? That is up to you. You can place just a few paving stones down the centre to act as a path, or cover the whole floor with paving. Some people feel that concrete over the whole floor of a small greenhouse makes an atmosphere too warm and dry and therefore they recommend excavating to a depth of 4 inch, and filling up with ½ inch stone chippings. This makes a floor that is both serviceable and attractive.

Pointing brickwork

But what about that other material that is so similar to concrete—mortar? This, of course, is the material you use for bricklaying but one important maintenance job you can tackle with it is to point the brickwork of your home. Well pointed brickwork is essential to the well-being of the structure of the house. If you let the pointing get too bad then, eventually I suppose, you could reach the stage where your house is no longer being held up. But long before that damp would be admitted.

So take a good look at your brickwork. Is the mortar in the joints between the bricks still in good condition? Or is it loose and crumbly, and have sections of it fallen away? If so, it is time you repointed. And this is just the sort of job on which the DIY man can save a lot of money by tackling himself, for it involves a lot of labour rather than a lot of expensive materials.

The first thing to do is take an old chisel, a hammer, and a wire brush, and prepare the brickwork. Rake out all loose material from the joints with a hammer and chisel and cut the mortar back to a depth of ½ inch. Then use the wire brush to remove anything still crumbly.

The mix for repointing is 1 of cement to 4 parts of soft sand, with very little water added—you need a really stiff consistency. The bricklayer then puts the mix on a hawk, and this is such a useful tool that it is worth your while improvising one. You need a piece of blockboard or plywood about 1 foot square, to the

STEPS IN RE-POINTING A WALL

1. Picking the mortar up from the hawk.
2. Pushing the mortar home into the vertical joints.
3. . . . then into the horizontals.
4. Trimming off the surplus.

underside of which you nail a handle—a length of broomstick, or a piece of 1 inch square softwood are both highly suitable. You also need a small pointing trowel. You will find it easier if you work on about 1 square yard of brickwork at a time, and I suggest you tackle all the vertical joints in this area first.

Hold the hawk, with the mortar on, close to the wall, pick up a piece of the mortar on the back of your trowel, push the mortar forward into the joint, tilting the front of your hawk upwards as you do, finally lifting the mortar clear. Hold the trowel at a slight angle as you press the mortar well in, and when you have finished a section of verticals chop off the thick surplus at the outside of each joint.

Complete the section by pointing the horizontals, in this case pressing the mortar home from the top of the joints. Fill each horizontal roughly, then draw your trowel across it to form a smooth continuous band of mortar. An ideal tool for cutting off the surplus mortar at the bottom of each joint can be improvised with an old kitchen knife. Sharpen the end of the knife to a point and bend it over. This tool, known to a bricklayer as a "frenchman", is drawn along a straightedge.

You can if you wish fill up each joint flush, but the more usual method is to have the mortar flush at the bottom but set in ¼ inch at the top, so that it slopes outwards. Thus any rainwater that gets in the joint will fall away and not linger about to soak into the brickwork. To ward off damp in an old house that does not have cavity walls, you can, after repointing and once you are sure the mortar has dried out properly, coat the whole of your house with a transparent waterproofing liquid.

14

Gardening under glass

GORDON COOPER

In the previous chapter Mike Smith described how to lay a concrete base for the greenhouse. Let us now look at gardening under glass generally—greenhouses, cold frames and cloches. This chapter is not an exhaustive treatment on how to treat different plants—it is a summary of the different types of growing under glass. As such I would like to start with a general observation.

Of all gardening and horticultural pastimes, growing under glass and particularly in a greenhouse is the most motivated. By this I mean that different people have different reasons for having a greenhouse and that no one has one for no reason. By contrast you could require a garden for no *horticultural* purpose whatsoever—just for your children to kick a ball around in, for example. If you require a greenhouse you need it for a purpose—and you must make up your mind what it is you want it for, before you purchase one. Is it for rare plants, i.e. a sort of challenge? Is it for tomatoes and other fine produce? Is it solely as an adjunct to your garden, i.e. for starting the half hardy annuals which you are later to plant out? Are you likely to expand, in your enthusiasm? Do you want heating installed? Will you want later to put heating in, even if you don't feel inclined to do so initially? Think hard about those things *first* and remember that a greenhouse and temperature that suits one plant will not suit another. You can't grow *everything* because you have a greenhouse.

I hope, incidentally that you are tempted to make a start. Of all gardening occupations, greenhousing is the least arduous and among the most enjoyable. Hardly gardening at all, really!

Two further things: firstly greenhouses, cold frames and cloches are not interchangeable nor do they do the same job. They are complementary in that a sequence, using first the greenhouse and then the frame or the cloches, can extend the growing season and the range of plants grown. Secondly, do not forget that a greenhouse can, quite simply, provide protection when and if you ever want it against extremes of climate. As well as for specific purposes it does also have this general capability, which is often overlooked.

What type of greenhouse

The "span roof" greenhouse is the most common model and certainly one of the most versatile. This type of house has sides which support a roof rising to a central ridge. When choosing make sure there is sufficient head room for you to work comfortably and for the plants to use. The span roof house may have glass to the ground on both sides or only one side. It may also have either wooden or brick walls for the bottom two feet or so. With glass-to-ground you can raise tall plants like tomatoes, with their roots in the soil or in pots, and once these are over you can use the space for winter flowering chrysanthemums. If they are grown in the border soil you can also grow lettuce as an intercrop.

For bedding and pot plants then the model with low walls may well be better as you can build staging all round and have a convenient working surface and display area. The space beneath the staging can be used for forcing rhubarb, bringing on bulbs and resting dormant plants. This space is also useful for over-wintering dahlias, begonias, geraniums, gladioli and other plants that need protection.

For tomatoes *and* pot plants, the model with a low wall on one side and glass to ground on the other is the one.

The "Lean-to" greenhouse is half a greenhouse fixed against a wall and if you have a south facing wall the heat provided can be remarkable as the wall itself throws heat into the house. The real merit of this style is the amount of head space available and the fact that there is a wall under glass against which you can raise grapes, peaches, nectarines or even exotic climbing plants.

A glance through any greenhouse manufacturer's catalogue will fascinate you by the variations that have been worked on these

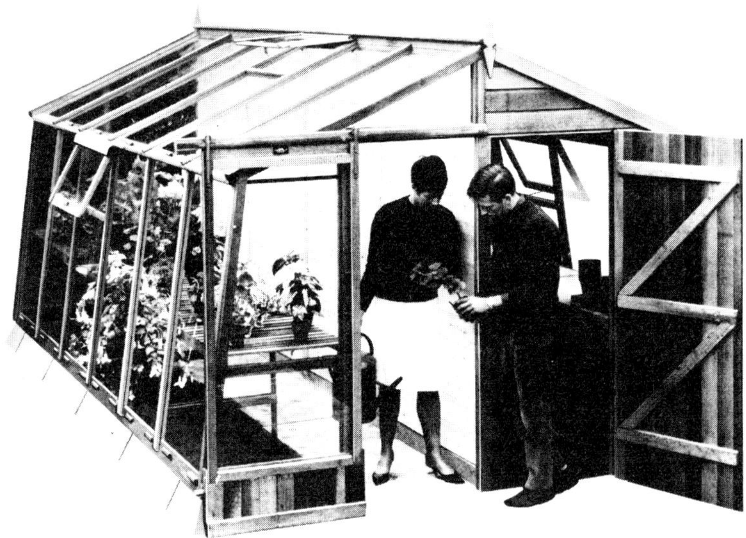

The span greenhouse may be glass-to-ground or built on a low wall. In this case the design incorporates a potting shed or workshop on one side.

three basic themes and you will find that there is a choice of basic constructional material. Some are made of cedar wood and these have the advantage of blending more sympathetically into a garden setting. As long as you get true cedar wood, it will need little maintenance apart from an occasional treatment with a wood preservative to keep the colour rich and warm. Soft wood greenhouses need regular painting. Metal frames mean more light for the plants and, moreover, aluminium or non-rusting frames involve no maintenance and give the longest life of all. But if you anticipate adding watering devices, shelves, polythene liners to save heat in the winter and any other gadgets that are fixed to the framework, this is more simply done with a wooden, rather than a metal frame.

Another point to consider before finally making up your mind is the greater cost of running a glass-to-ground model through the winter. The final but important consideration is ventilation, for there must be a flow of air.

Heating a greenhouse

Now don't forget that it doesn't *have* to be heated—what is known as a "cold" greenhouse can be very useful. If you like, also, you can partition the greenhouse so that part is cool and part is heated. This is something to bear in mind when buying—see how extensions can be fitted. (Incidentally, plan to add your extension on the end which has the door. Then it is a comparatively simple matter and what was previously the outside door becomes the partition door.)

Whether heating part or whole, it can be costly. Just pause and think how much heat would be required for you to be able to sit out in the greenhouse in moderate comfort during a freezing January evening. If you consider Mike Smith's discussion of double glazing in the chapter *Insulating the home* and reflect that you are sitting in a room that is *all* glass . . . Clearly, the cost would be immense. If you *must* grow bananas, however, I suppose you are sufficiently obsessed to put in hot water pipes, steam valves for humidity and all, with a great solid fuel boiler—hard work but much the cheapest form of heating—and if you want to go in for a penny, I might as well give you a push for a pound. And I would think that any other form of heating would be out of the question from a cost point of view.

The last is just an extreme illustration, perhaps, so let's get back to reality and consider all the forms of heating—paraffin, electricity, solid fuel, gas and, most important of all, the sun. In general remember that the temperature you maintain on the coldest night is the determining factor.

Siting the greenhouse. A sunny spot is clearly essential, free from overhanging trees and shadows cast by either trees or buildings. It should be as close to the house as possible especially if you are going to run electricity or water into the greenhouse itself. If you are concentrating on growing plants in the winter then your greenhouse should run east to west while north to south is better for summer crops. For general purposes north to south is best.

Electricity. This is the one for versatility—once it is laid on there are all those lovely attachments to make the job of running the greenhouse almost automatic, from watering right through to insect control.

Putting the electricity through to the greenhouse is a job for a professional and your electricity board will be happy to advise on this. Heating can be either by tubular heater, immersion heater and four inch water pipes working from an adapted solid fuel boiler, or fan assisted heaters that blow warm air and provide both heat and air circulation. Electric heat is ideal in that it is clean and safe.

Paraffin. Simple to work and cheap to both install and run, the paraffin heater works well as long as it is kept immaculately clean. Paraffin fumes are harmful to plants and as paraffin when burned puts extra moisture into the air, ventilation becomes even more important. Buy one of the models made especially for greenhouses, as this reduces the danger from fumes and also incorporates tubes to spread the heat over as wide an area as possible.

Solid fuel. Very efficient and the cheapest to run. Care must be taken in siting the boiler as changes in wind direction can change the rate of burning. Regular stoking is required; this and the maintenance of pipes and boilers explain the declining popularity.

Gas heating. In the past gas fired boilers have been unpopular because their fumes could be harmful to plants but the advent of natural gas and new designs of heater make this criticism no longer valid. The Gas Board have recently introduced a model which could well interest many greenhouse owners for its simplicity and efficiency.

The cold greenhouse. Plants must be hardy. Rock plants (alpines), camellias, rhododendrons, azaleas, heathers and spring flowering shrubs will grow well and you can also grow bulbs and summer bedding plants under glass. As there is no additional heat these last will not flower much earlier than in the open garden.

The cool greenhouse. With a temperature of 40°–45°F the scope of the greenhouse increases dramatically. Carnations, cacti, orchids (i.e. cymbidium), cinerarias, primulas, pelargoniums, coleus, ferns and the half hardy seeds can all be raised and grown successfully. This increased heat means that really hardy plants like the alpines cannot be grown in the same house.

The warm greenhouse. Temperature must be maintained at 48°–55°F. I recommend some of the African violets and cyclamen among other more exotic plants; and there is the additional pleasure of forcing some out of season vegetable crops—lettuce, tomatoes, french beans and strawberries are quite practical. You can also compete with your local florists once you keep up this sort of heat.

The hot greenhouse. The hothouse needs a temperature of

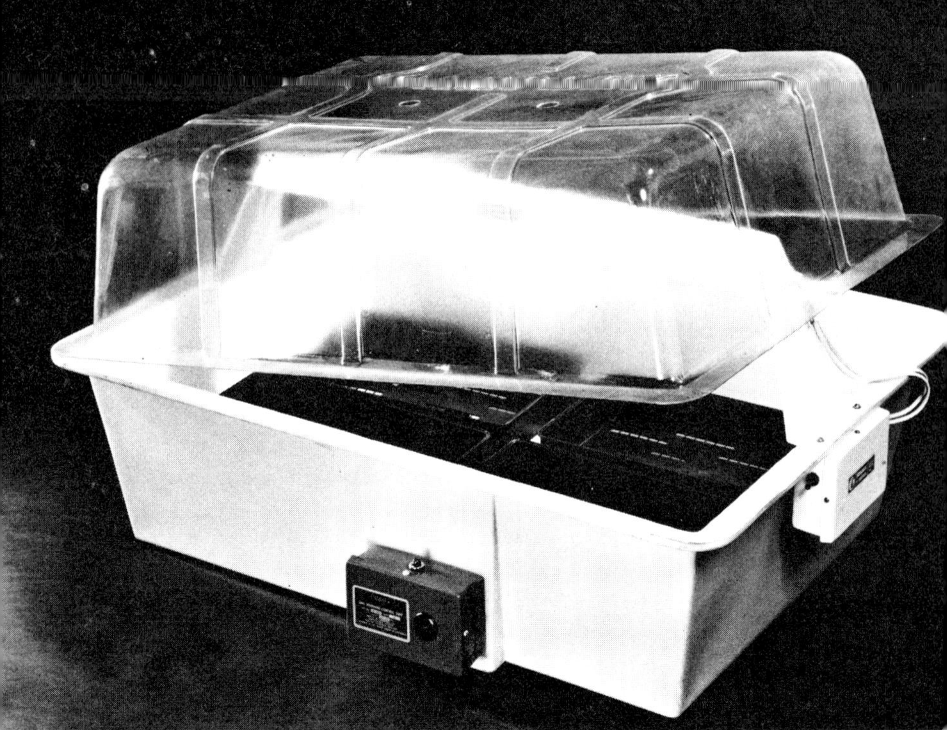

This propagating frame has an electric element with thermostatic control in the base but heating can be provided by a small paraffin heater or even an electric light bulb in smaller models.

60°–65°F and is for the real enthusiast who will pay as much or more for his fuel as he does for his plants. Tropical plants like crotons, anthuriums, gardenias, bananas, pineapples and out of season cucumbers find a home here.

Propagating frames

A propagating frame is like a small garden frame. With it you can raise the temperature of a small area instead of increasing the heat throughout the greenhouse. By doing this you will get cuttings to root more easily and persuade seeds to germinate that would not do so at normal temperatures. The frame itself is a two part construction with a base to accommodate a heating element and a transparent cover to maintain a humid atmosphere in which the plants thrive.

The heating element can be anything from a 40 watt light bulb under a seed tray to sophisticated electric cables running through the soil itself. With the latter, the whole base may be warmed or just a part of it and the controls on the unit will enable you to vary the temperature according to the needs of the plants you are raising; a built-in thermostat regulates this temperature. (You will note that this is one of those useful accessories which only electricity can supply.)

Even with just bulb-warmed soil, which costs less than the price of a cigarette a day to run, you will be able to get dahlias, fuchsias and chrysanthemums to make roots quickly, and many of those half-hardy plants that take a while to germinate without bottom heat can be brought on.

Use a John Innes compost in your propagating frame as this is sterilised so that weeds seeds will not be a problem once germination starts. In the same way it is worth avoiding trouble by watering the compost with Cheshunt Compound as a precaution against damping off.

Cold frames

While not taking the place of greenhouses the cold frame is an essential part of the garden cycle and has its own functions in hardening off plants raised in the greenhouse as well as being used for rooting cuttings, growing salad crops, overwintering small plants, growing cucumbers or melons or even housing your collection of alpine plants.

Frames come in two styles, the "span" which is rather like two frames back to back and the "lean-to" which is the single frame, taller at the back than at the front. The glass covers, called "lights", can be either large sheets (Dutch lights) or smaller overlapping panes on a solid but not too heavy framework of glazing bars.

At one time all frames were cold frames and in severe weather additional frost protection was obtained by laying sacking over the lights. Today, by using underground electrically-heated cables a useful soil temperature can be maintained. If this heating is extended around the walls of the frame then the air temperature can be raised so that, particularly on span-type models, you have almost got an additional greenhouse.

When siting the frame choose a sunny spot close to the greenhouse. Make sure the site is well drained and, if there is danger of cold winds, put a low fence or screen around the windward

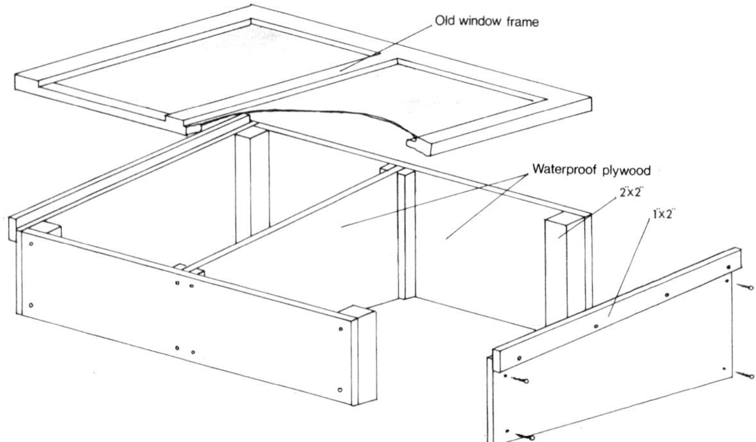

An easily made cold frame.

side. By putting the frame close to the greenhouse you cut down the carrying and you will also be able to use the water and electricity provided for the greenhouse with only minimal extensions. Ventilate by opening the frame whenever practical, even in the winter for a few hours; in summer, light shade from the hot sun prevents the plants burning off.

Making your own cold frame

If you can get hold of an old window from a demolition contractor, then building a cold frame for your garden becomes a very simple inexpensive matter. The four sides can consist of exterior quality plywood, ½ inch thick, and they are joined with butt joints, glued and screwed (always use waterproof materials). To strengthen the construction, pegs are inserted at all internal corners—these should be of 2×2 inch for the main corners, but 1 inch square will do where the centre divider meets the main frame. The window merely sits on top of the frame, but lengths of 2×1 inch timber are fixed to the sides to form a channel in which the window can run. If there is a tendency for the window to slide off because the sides of the frame slope (this is necessary, incidentally, so that rainwater will drain away) then another length of 2×1 could be fixed at the bottom end.

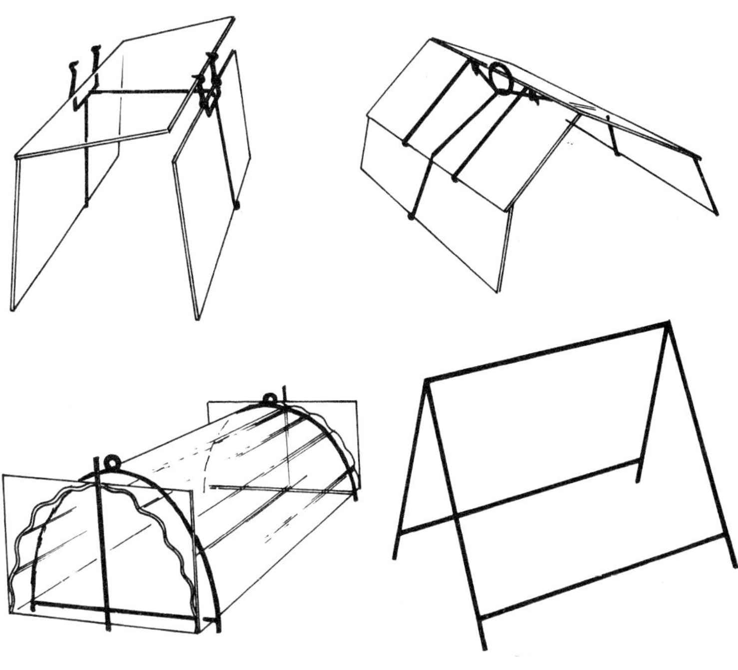

In addition to individual cloches, row protection is provided by joining them together or using polythene on wire supports.

Cloches

The simplest form of glass protection, the cloche is simply pieces of glass held together either with clips or a special framework of wires. Some cloche structures are quite ambitious, using several panes of glass, and these can be used for the taller growing plants. A line of cloches can provide cover the length of the seed bed and polythene cloches are available to do this also. With a cloche, vegetables get away to a good start and give you an earlier harvest. The protection gives better germination, so sowing should be thinner than in the open garden. The variety of seed you choose should be one that matures quickly and will be hardy enough to put up with the occasional touch of low temperature—inevitable when raising plants in the early stages of the year.

15

Containers for gardening

GORDON COOPER

If you have a small garden or a yard with no soil, or are considering building yourself that patio described by Mike Smith in Chapter 12, or just fancy a bit of colour right outside your kitchen window, then much pleasure and creative gardening can be had by using containers of one sort or another—a window box is the item which comes immediately to mind. There is all the pleasure of growing plants and little of the gardener's usual hard work. For older people there is also the fact that the level of the soil is raised, so that bending is no longer necessary.

It is obviously not a skill separate from general gardening but there are several special points that need considering. For example, the amount of soil per plant in any container is far less than the volume available to a plant in the open garden and for this reason feeding and watering must be watched much more carefully.

What sort of container

But before starting on culture of the plants themselves, let us consider the containers. The window box comes in all sorts of sizes and materials, from wood through to metal and fibreglass, with decorative designs cast into the walls of the box. All of them are satisfactory, of course, but there is an additional pleasure in making it yourself for your window. Opposite is a plan for construction, supplied by Mike Smith; plus another for the construction of a heavier garden tub (see p. 125).

Window boxes can go anywhere around the house but obviously, if they are made as fixtures, the colder sides will have the hardier

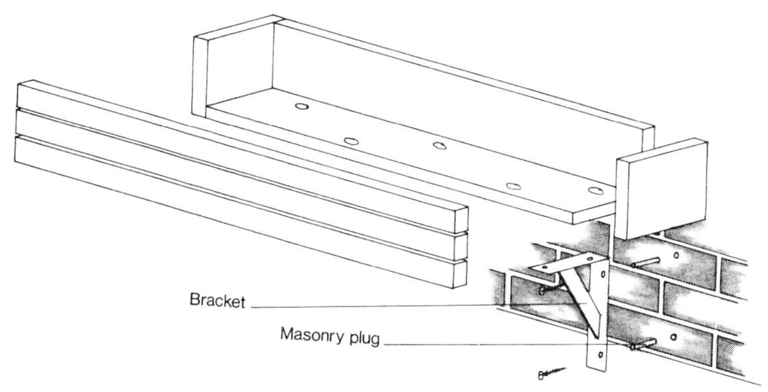

FLOWER CONTAINER

A flower box has to stand up to a certain amount of rough treatment—from the weather, the pressure of the soil inside it, even the action of the plant roots. It is as well, therefore, to make it fairly sturdy. All the timber should be ideally 1 inch, although you might get away with $\frac{3}{4}$ inch. Its required width—which, of course, will determine the internal dimensions of the box—will depend on what you want to grow, but it should be at least 6 inch, and preferably 8 or 9 inch. The construction can be entirely of butt joints, provided you cut all the timber true and square to make the meeting surface as large as possible, but the pieces should be glued together, as well as being nailed, using waterproof adhesive and non-rusting nails. Holes are bored in the bottom for drainage, and so that these do not get blocked up cover them with a layer of broken crocks. The front of this box has been given a decorative feature in the shape of two grooves. These can be ploughed out with a grooving plane, or a power saw. If you do not possess either of these tools, you can create the grooves artificially by pinning narrow strips of moulding on to a backing piece of ordinary timber. The box is shown as being supported on two ordinary shelf brackets, screwed into wall plugs. Make sure that all the fixings are firm and secure—you do not want to risk having the box fall down and cause damage or injury. Often, of course, flower boxes are placed on window ledges. In that case they should be held securely in place by chain. The interior of the box should be treated with a preservative that will not harm plant life, and all the rest painted.

plants. Tubs, troughs and other free-standing containers can be positioned with greater freedom. Imagination is the only limit to the container you use: tubs, barrels cut in half, hollow tree trunks, wooden boxes, plastic boxes, concrete dishes, old wheel barrows, wooden wheels laid flat with the space between the spokes filled with soil, and almost anything that will hold compost and take drainage holes.

Old sinks in particular make good homes for a collection of small alpine plants and a few carefully chosen rocks. The glaze on the sink needs covering: a mixture of 2½ parts sand, 1 part cement and 1½ parts peat (called Hyper-tufa) gives an effect remarkably like sandstone when spread on top of the glaze. To make it stick you first paint the area to be treated with a bonding agent like Polybond and then apply the mixture while it is still tacky. Small containers can be given an added sense of style by fixing brass carrying handles.

Soil for containers

When all is ready, put broken crocks along the bottom for drainage. This is vital. The soil must be moist but no plant will grow in a waterlogged container. This will allow the moisture through but stop the soil going with it. Now about this soil. Ordinary garden soil put straight into containers is not really satisfactory. Quite simply it is not well-balanced enough. As you will not need a great amount for your containers, it will pay you to buy sterilised John Innes compost, as this will not have weed seed in it and contains the balance of food, peat, chalk and loam that get the plants off to a good start and keeps them growing well. Do not completely fill the container, but leave ½ inch at the top to allow easy watering. And one final little point here—a container filled with soil can be heavy so, if it is a big one, make sure it's in the position you finally intend before you put the compost in!

Gardeners who have a number of containers to fill make up their own compost as this can be less expensive than buying it ready mixed. The job is over and done with if you make a year's supply at a time, and the old compost can go onto the garden as a top dressing when the boxes are replanted. If you make your own compost, try a proven blend of Loam (7 parts), Peat (3 parts), Sand (2 parts), Chalk (¾ ozs per bushel) and John Innes Base (¼ lb. per bushel from your Garden Centre).

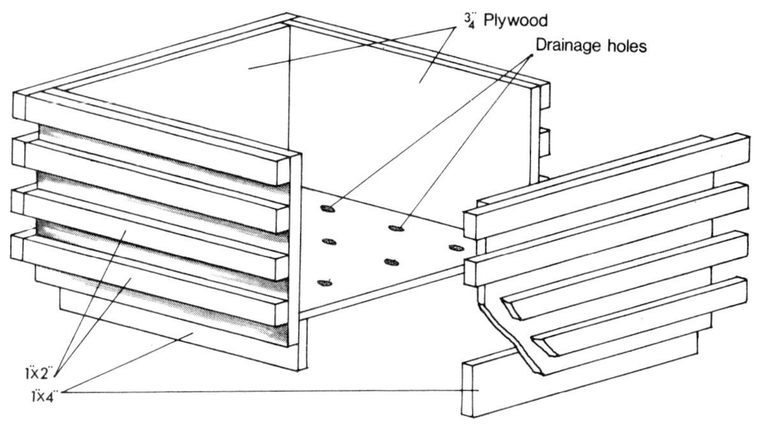

GARDEN TUB

Attractive tubs in which to grow plants can be quite expensive to buy, so it is worth while making this one shown here. The tub needs to be of robust construction, so use exterior grade plywood (in fact, it might even be worth buying marine ply—the stuff that boat hulls are made from) waterproof glue, and non-rusting nails. Cut the four sides squarely and true, so that there will be as large a meeting surface as possible, from $\frac{3}{4}$ inch plywood, and glue and pin them together. Fit lengths of 4×1 inch timber to the inside of the box, so that just half protrudes, to form a plinth. The $\frac{3}{4}$ inch plywood bottom of the box, into which drainage holes are bored, sits on this plinth. Strips of 2×1 inch timber are fixed to the outside of the box as a decorative feature, and are spaced at 2 inch intervals. The box will thus be 16 inch tall—or slightly under, because timber that is nominally 2 inch wide will, in fact, be just less. An internal dimension of 2 foot $\times$ 2 foot is suitable. As with the flower box on page 00, the interior of the tub should be treated with a preservative that will not harm plant life, and all the rest painted. Cover the bottom with crocks to stop the drainage holes from getting blocked before you put in any soil.

Planting and aftercare

Planting your container is a matter of choice. Seeds, bulbs, bedding plants, small shrubs, miniature roses are all possible and depend largely on the depth of soil you are going to provide. Dwarf fruit trees and clematis do well, while camellias, magnolias and small rhododendrons flourish under these conditions provided the soil is free of lime or chalk. There are no rules about what you can grow and what you can't. If you feel inclined to try something then go right ahead, you may get some splendid effects. A particular hint: don't forget trailing plants. Apart from their intrinsic appeal, they can be used for hiding an unsightly support or an ugly feature of your container.

The soil must be kept moist but not waterlogged: in dry spells plants will use more water and even if there is rain about you may still need to water. Once the plants start to droop they need water but they do not benefit from flooding. Your window boxes need watching particularly; in many cases they will be beneath the eaves of the house and will not collect rain water. Use tepid water as cold tap water on a hot day can set back root growth. For feeding, use either a liquid fertiliser or a granulated compound fertiliser such as you use on the open garden, watered in after application. Remember to keep it off the leaves or it may scorch them.

16

The compost heap

GORDON COOPER

Is your "compost heap" just a pile of evil-smelling rubbish, which you poke from time to time and wonder why the contents so little resemble what you have been lead to expect? Before we turn to planning and looking after your garden in the next section let us take a look at that too often neglected but so useful commodity—compost.

First—what does and does not go into the heap. You will, of course have the usual heap of burnable rubbish from the garden, but this should be close to the bonfire or incinerator site. On this heap will go all the prunings, dead wood and other indisposable matter that will not rot down to become compost, together with couch grass, bindweed and other vicious perennial weeds for which burning is the only fate.

A true compost heap absorbs grass cuttings, annual weeds, dead flowers, leaves, vegetable tops, light hedge trimmings, tea leaves, orange peel, straw and all other waste vegetable matter. These should be in regular layers. A proprietary "activator", it is generally agreed, is then added, to encourage the breaking down of the vegetable waste into usable compost. Added soil also provides the bacteria needed for such breaking down and, furthermore, layers of soil also cut down the smell, which some find offensive.

The best compost heaps are built up layer by layer, each one six to nine inches thick. These should be firmed down by treading and if at all dry it should be watered before adding the "activator" and soil layer. If you use an activator, follow the maker's instructions. (Incidentally, chicken manure and sulphate of ammonia

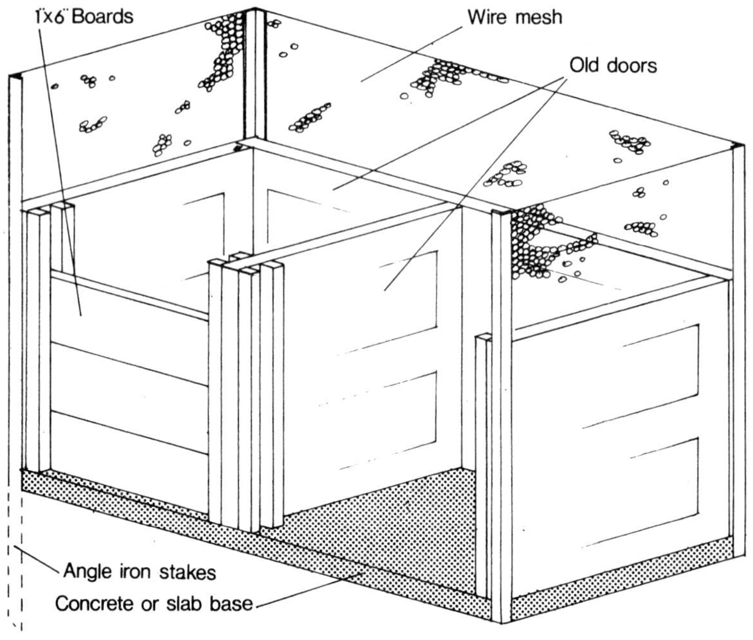

A compost bunker you can make.

can also be used for this job.)

When your heap has reached the right height, add a few inches of soil all over the top to retain the heat which the compost generates and to speed up the decomposition process. Make sure that the heap does not dry out, as the breaking down process is a combination of heat and moisture. I suppose I should add that ideally you should protect the heap from getting too wet but, ideal as it is, I can't deny that few gardeners bother about this—neither do I blame them! It will be about six months before your heap will be ready for use and the compost should be a rick dark brown, like peat, and should have a lovely, clean, earthy smell.

Making a bunker

You must have a firm base of concrete or slabs, to make it easier to use. Find space for two heaps, one beside the other; in this way you can use the compost from one while building the second. The walls must be firm and can be built of railway sleepers;

bricks with an opening at the front into which extra wooden slats can be dropped as the depth of the heap increases; corrugated iron or chicken wire supported by strong stakes.

But rather than such general instructions, you may like to follow this neat, simple idea of Mike Smith's. It is made up from old doors—you can usually snap them up at demolition sites. The doors sit on a concrete base (see Chapter 13 for details of how to build this) and are held in place by angle-iron stakes driven into the ground.

The dividing partition is nailed to the door that forms the back; at the front it can be held by a stake driven into the ground, or you could use an angle bracket on each side to fix it to plugs of timber let into the concrete whilst you were constructing the base. The bunker is topped off with mesh. Fix this to the angle iron with nuts and bolts that pass through holes you will have to drill. At the front of the bunker, lengths of 1 inch square timber are nailed to the doors to form chanelling in which you drop 6 × 1 inch boards, to keep the compost from spilling out at the front. The boards are easily removed when eventually you need to shovel rotted compost out.

17

Repairs to fencing

MIKE SMITH

The thing about dilapidated fencing is that it looks so awful. Some people do find the prospect of repairs rather daunting, however, so I hope this chapter will at least set out clearly how to do what needs to be done.

Good care begins the minute you take over a brand new fence. Your first task must be to see that it is properly treated with preservative—if it is you should get upwards of 25 years' service from a well-built fence. Some woods, such as cedar and larch, have their own natural resistance to decay but these are very expensive timbers and it is more than likely that your fence will be built of something cheaper that does require protection.

The best protection of all is offered by a factory applied preservative and it pays you in the first place to buy your materials from one of the specialist suppliers who offer timber that has been so treated. Even so, subsequent maintenance will still be necessary but what you have to do will depend on the type of treatment as well as the type of timber, so be sure always to follow the supplier's instructions.

If you are starting off with raw timber, then one of the most popular, and the cheapest, of fence preservatives is creosote, which is easily applied by brush. Give your fence two or three coats of creosote, allowing each one to soak in thoroughly before you apply the next. Certain points of a fence are especially vulnerable, so be very liberal at such points with your application of creosote, or indeed any preservative. These points are where the rails (the horizontal members to which the boards are actually nailed) enter the posts; the whole of the bottom rail; the part of the boards below the bottom rail where they are nearest to the ground; and the lower parts of the post. Try, too, to force the preservative down the back of the boards, where they are covered by the rails.

Creosote is, however, ineffective below ground, so apply a proprietary preservative that is recommended for such use to the part of a post that is buried and, indeed, for the first 6 inch protruding above the soil. Ideally, this part of the post should be stood in a drum of preservative and left to soak for 24 hours. Since such treatment is likely to be beyond the resources of the average householder, an alternative is to try to soak at least the very end of the post. At that most vulnerable point of all, the inch or so immediately above and below the soil level, make a ring of indentations with a hammer and cold chisel. These indentations will help the preservative to soak in better.

Remember that creosote and some other preservatives will burn the skin, so always wear gloves when using them, keep your arms covered and look out for splashes on your face.

One other obvious preservative is paint but you will have to give your fence the very thorough treatment of primer, undercoat and two top coats, so it can work out expensive. Furthermore, it does not soak into the wood and if any chips off and leaves bare patches, then your fence is not getting protection at that point. And applying paint is a much more time-consuming, painstaking job than brushing on creosote. I would advise you to use paint only if you must.

Repairs

If your fence is a few years old, take a look at it to see if it needs any running repairs. With a bit of luck you might catch these in time before they develop into something serious. One of the most common of minor faults will be that the boards have worked loose—strong winds or climbing children may have caused the nails to spring free. Take out the old nails, and replace them with new ones driven in at a fresh spot. Use galvanised nails where possible. These last longer, and, furthermore, there will be no rust stains to disfigure attractive timber.

Now run your eye over the general line of the fence, to check whether it is sagging or leaning. If it is, try to trace the cause. One

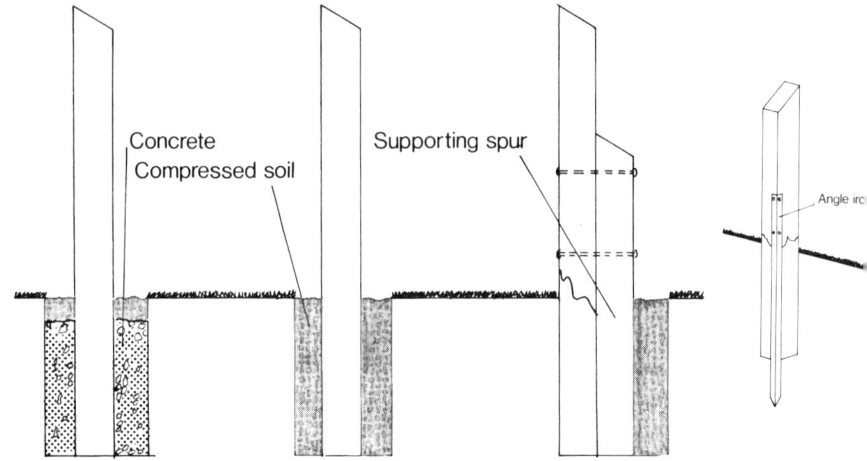

MAKING SURE A FENCE POST IS WELL SUPPORTED
1. A post supporting a heavy fence should be cemented in.
2. . . . otherwise well-compacted soil will do.
3. A rotted post needs to be supported by a spur.
4. . . . or else a length of angle iron.

of the most likely reasons will be that the post has been pulled out of true. Check the post at soil level and below, hacking out any sign of rot, and dousing the affected parts with preservative. The post might be so badly decayed that it needs reinforcing. This can be done with a concrete or wooden spur sunk about 2 foot into the ground, and bolted to about 18 inch of sound post above the ground. Less obtrusive is the use of metal plates or angle iron bolted to sound timber above and below the rotten section, or bolted to the post above ground and sunk into concrete.

If the post is in a really bad state, then it should be pulled out and replaced. I'll tell you a quick and easy way of pulling out an old fence post. Bore a hole into it, and jam in a crow bar or similar steel rod. Place a car jack under the bar, raise the jack and it will lift the post out of the ground. If the post is so rotten that it snaps as it is being pulled out, then you will have to dig the stump out. When buying a new post choose timber of the same size as the old, so that it will match the rest of the fence.

Putting in posts

A post from 3–6 feet high should be sunk from 2 feet to 2 feet

6 inches into the soil, depending on how firm the ground is, and how heavy the fence it has to support. A taller post should go even further into the ground. Dump about 3 inches of rubble or gravel into the bottom of the hole and compact it down firmly. Now insert the post and ram in another 6 inches of gravel or soil, so that it holds the post upright. Check with a plumb line or spirit level that the post is truly upright in all directions then brace it with struts nailed to the top of the post and to stakes drive into the ground. Now you can fill in the hole. If the horizontal rails are jointed into the post, then the rail may well have to be inserted before you push the post fully home into the hole.

It is not a bad idea to concrete-in a post that has to support a very heavy fence in an exposed position. Start off with a 3 inch bed or gravel in just the same way—if you poured concrete directly onto the base of the hole, it would interfere with drainage, and there would be damp soil around the base of the post, threatening it with rot.

As you fill the hole with concrete check its alignment with your spirit level or pumb line and brace it within half an hour of pouring in the concrete—you can't wriggle the post around once the concrete starts to harden. Slope the top of the concrete away from the post so that rainwater will run away.

If the post is set in concrete, wait a week for the concrete to set before you nail on the cladding, but otherwise you can begin right away. Once again you ought to use galvanized nails, so that they will not rust.

Incidentally, you will notice that all the really hard work associated with putting up new fencing has been completed when the posts are cemented or compacted into the ground. This is particularly the case if you intend to use lap-fencing supplied or made up into large panels. Provided the height and distance between posts are correct, then hey presto! Opposite are some illustrated examples.

Replacing rails

If the rails of your fence are rotten, then these should be replaced. This can be quite a tricky operation should the rails be jointed into the posts and you will probably find that there is nothing for it but to pull up at least one of the posts to which a rotting rail is fixed. True there are all kinds of makeshift methods, such as using metal brackets or scraps of timber to hold the rail to the post, but you cannot expect fencing constructed like this to give your home a neat and trim appearance.

First remove all the cladding boards from the rotten rail, saw through it where it is tenoned into the post, then use a mallet and chisel (preferably an old one for there may be nails around to damage it) to remove the stubs of the rails from the sockets in the post. Before you insert the new rail, soak its end and front, plus the socket of the post, with preservative, for these are the spots difficult to reach when the fence is constructed.

Drive nails (once again choose a non-rusting kind if you can get them) through the posts and into the rail. Now you can fix the cladding boards back in place, discarding any that are defective and replacing them with new ones.

Minor jobs you can do on a fence that seems to be in perfect trim are to clear away any soil that may have piled up against the baseboard and inspect climbing plants and shrubs for any growth that may force open joints or crevices. In the spring apply a weedkiller along the gap at the bottom of the fence.

Finally, resolve to save yourself all this work in future by applying a preservative every two or three years.

18

Birds, water and comfort

MIKE SMITH

Let us close this section of the book—a section too full of hard work, you may well complain—with a bit of creative comfort for all creatures. Here are plans and advice on a bird-nesting box, a fish pond, with or without a fountain and a garden seat.

Nesting box

Here is the basic idea. I will not be too specific about sizes of materials, because for this sort of construction you can use up a lot of leftovers from previous jobs. You will probably have to buy the pole, and this should be something like 2½ inch square. Set it in the ground in a way similar to the methods described for fencing (Chapter 17).

The feeding tray consists of a sheet of exterior grade plywood, with a lipping of thin timber, into which it is a good idea to bore a drain hole. Cut a square hole in the centre of the sheet, and slip the tray over the top of the post. It is held in position by four wedge shaped pieces of timber, mortised into the post. Higher up the post drill holes and insert a length of dowelling that forms perches for the birds.

The nesting area is built up from three triangular pieces that sit on, and are fixed to, a base. A series of feather-edge boards are fixed to the triangular pieces to form the roof, and at the ridge of the roof are two capping pieces. Try to make the joint between these two a good fit so that it will be waterproof, although you could seal it with a mastic if you wish.

The birds get into the nesting area through holes bored into the

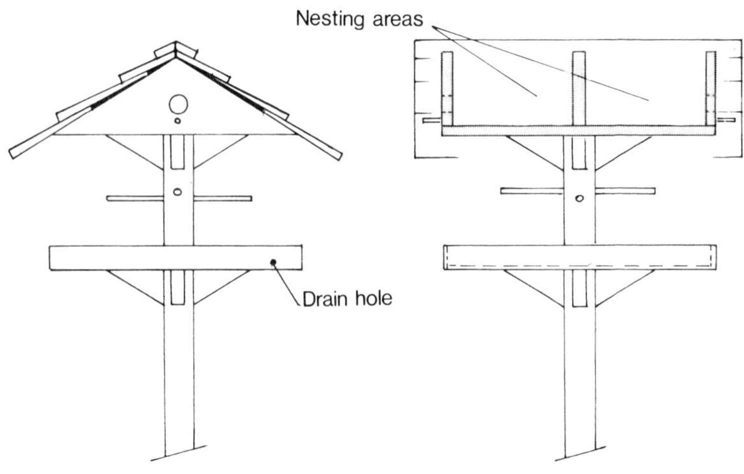

A nesting box for birds.

two end triangular pieces, and a dowel peg is fixed in place to create another perch immediately below this opening.

Once again, as with the feeding tray, four triangular supports, fixed to the post, support the base, and thus hold the whole nesting area in place.

Ponds and fountains

Not nearly as difficult as you might think—and obviously very pretty. First for the pond—you can always stop there if you wish. The simplest and cheapest way is to dig a hole and line it with polythene—but be sure to buy a grade that is recommended for such use. Your pool may then not be such a permanent structure as one lined with concrete, or one that uses a pre-cast fibreglass mould. But it will nevertheless give you years of service, although it is quick and cheap to construct.

All you do is dig a hole to whatever shape you wish, but creating two or three different levels, and trying to give it attractive contours. Of course, the hole should not be so big that you cannot cover it with one sheet of liner. Line the bottom of the pool with soft sand first, then place the polythene in the hole. At first it must be very loose—make no attempt to follow the shape of the pool. Now slowly fill the pool up with water, the pressure

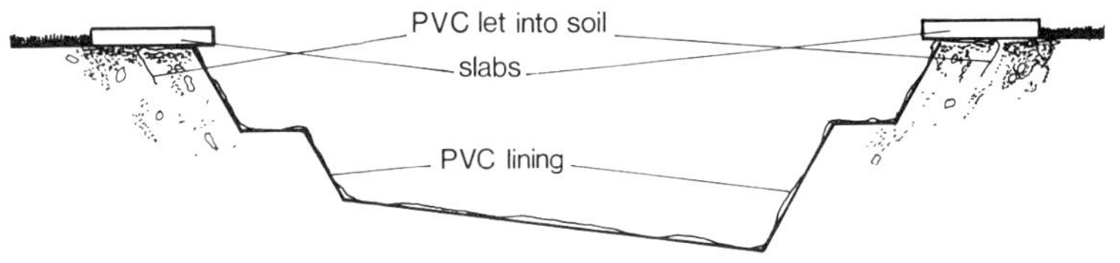

of which will mould the polythene to the shape of the hole.

The top ends of the polythene are held in place under 1 foot square concrete paving slabs, which you can either buy or make yourself (see Chapter 12).

A small fountain

The principles of installing a small fountain are these. You buy what is known as a submersible pump, i.e. one that can be safely placed under water. This you plunge into your pool, connect it to an electricity supply and switch on. And you have your fountain. The arrangement is perfectly safe, for the submersible pump is fully insulated and designed for such an operation. It sucks up water from the pool and throws it up into the air; the water falls back into the pool to be used once again for the fountain. Thus the system is what is known as re-circulatory—in other words no water is introduced from outside.

And that is all there is to it. Well . . . almost. For in practice one or two refinements are needed. For a start when you buy your pump you may well find that the outlet from it is just an open pipe and to get an attractive spray a fountain jet will have to be fitted. Fountain kits, consisting of a submersible pump and a jet, can be bought.

Then again your pool may well be too deep for you to place your pump on the bottom—the jet, too, would be submerged. In that case, you must build a small platform to stand it on. This can consist of bricks merely placed on top of each other—no mortar is needed, although it is as well to bond them in some form. For instance, if the area of your platform were to consist of two bricks side by side, then the second course should lie across the first one, and so on. It is perfectly permissible to construct a platform for the pump in a pool built with a plastic liner—you run little risk of tearing the liner. You will probably, however, want to take a little more care in placing your first course of bricks than you would if you were building on concrete.

Finally, you will probably find that your pump has a fairly short electrical lead—nowhere near long enough to reach your house, where the point is. To extend it you must use only the appropriate weatherproof materials, and if you are in any doubt about your ability to carry out the work, ask an electrician to do it for you. The lead from your pump is joined up to the extra cable by means of a waterproof connector, and the whole run is then buried under soil so that it will be less likely to be damaged. It is a good idea to have the cable connector easily accessible—hidden under a stone at the side of the pool, for instance—so that you can remove the pump at any time without having to uproot the whole cable run, thus disturbing your garden. At the house end, the cable can then be plugged in to any convenient three-pin socket outlet.

But let's get back to the fountain. The arrangement I have described is perfectly workable, but in fact all manner of design possibilities open up before you; a wide range of jets is available, and the water need not emerge merely from a jet just above the water. You can also buy all manner of statues and ornaments to which a fountain jet is fixed. At this stage, remember that one of the most important design elements is the power of the pump. If the pump isn't strong enough you might be disappointed, so always discuss your plans and requirements thoroughly with the man who sells you the materials.

A waterfall

Of course, a fountain is not the only means of introducing moving water into your pool. You can also have a waterfall. The principles of these are very similar—once again a submersible pump can be at the heart of things. You need, of course, raised ground at the side of your pool, and a series of "steps" leading down to it. These you can fashion yourself out of concrete, or buy rock-like cascade effects in plastics.

The pump is sited in the pool close to the bottom of the waterfall. Tubing is used to carry the water to the top of the fall, so that it can cascade back through the "steps" and into the main pool. The tube, of course, is buried so that it cannot be seen.

Once again, you can buy complete waterfall kits, and it is possible to get pumps that will supply both a waterfall and a fountain. Remember, again, that the scale of your design must be matched up to the ability of your pump to carry enough water to the top.

Incidentally, I do not want you to get the idea from reading this that submersible pumps are the only kind that can be used for fountains and waterfalls. Surface pumps are made, too, and these have to be sited outside the pool in some form of housing. Essentially they are more powerful and used for more ambitious designs. Obviously, they are more expensive. I suggest you start with the submersible type.

One final thing: fountains are good for pond life, both fishy and otherwise, as the water is thereby aerated.

A garden seat

Like the patio table, this is pretty straightforward in its construction.

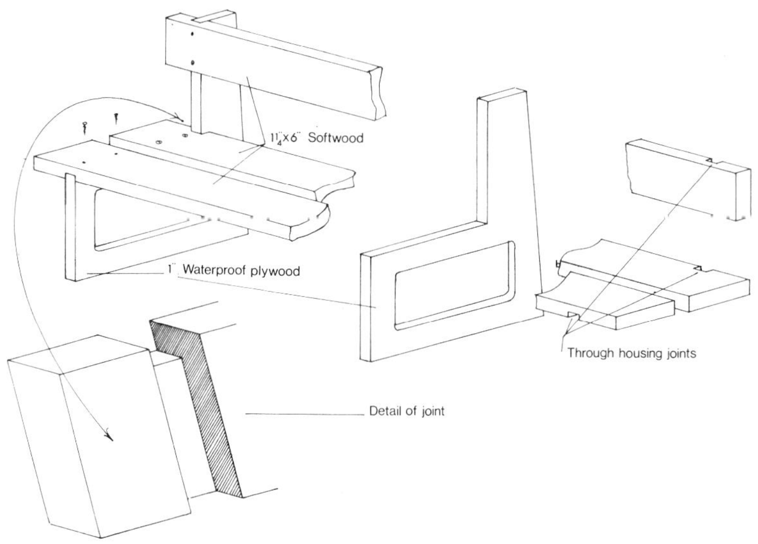

GARDEN SEAT

Attractive exterior furniture enhances any garden or patio, and here is a seat that it should not be too difficult for a woodworker with some experience to make. The sides are cut from 1 inch exterior grade plywood. It can be difficult to buy plywood of this thickness, but anything less would not be strong enough, so if you cannot get it locally, I suggest you buy two sheets of ½ inch plywood, and fix them together, using a waterproof glue. The construction would not be strong enough if the 6 × 1¼ inch planks of the seat and the back merely lay flat on the sides, and were just screwed in place. Accordingly simply housing joints are used. The inset detail shows the joint needed where the seat meets the back upright. All the joints should be strengthened with waterproof glue and non-rusting screws. The finished seat can be painted, but if you want a natural finish treat it with a preservative suitable for use out of doors.

PART 3 JOBS IN THE GARDEN

19

How to dig

GORDON COOPER

No, I'm afraid there is nothing for it—we all have to dig. It is the basis of gardening, which is why I start this garden section with some hints.

Depending on how you look at it digging can be pleasant exercise or damned hard work. Now often it is hard work simply because it is not planned correctly or the spade or fork is badly used or it is done at the wrong time of the year when soil conditions and weather are against you. After a break, take it easy. You will be using muscles that have not had a lot of exercise for months and a violent attack on heavy soil can leave you stiff and aching for days. Incidentally, let me remind you of my earlier words extolling the bliss of stainless steel tools. Can you possibly afford a spade and fork in this sweetest of metals?

The best time for digging over large areas of soil is late autumn or early winter, especially on heavy soils, although plenty of digging is done in the early spring and on light soil this is to be preferred as it avoids the consolidation that a wet winter can cause. By doing the job before the worst of the weather sets in your soil will still be workable, you can leave the soil ridged, and the winter snow and frosts will help break it down to a granular structure.

Why dig at all? It is an opportunity to work organic materials into the soil, it helps with soil drainage and allows the air into the soil which keeps the bacteria working. Some gardeners avoid the job all together and keep the soil live by adding a layer of compost over the soil in the autumn and then sowing seeds into this compost in the spring. Another method is to simply sow the seeds in the spring and cover them with a couple of inches of compost. You will need a lot of compost and it has been calculated that it runs at about 4 or 5 tons for the average sized garden of 30 feet by 40 feet. Much of that is under grass, of course, but you'll still need about two tons—better start planning where the lorry is to dump it!

For most of us, however, digging is an integral part of the gardening year and there are three basic techniques—Single digging, Double digging and Ridging.

Single digging

For most gardeners on established plots, single digging is all that is needed. This involves turning the soil over to the depth of the spade (called a "spit"). As with other digging methods, the first step is to take out a trench and lay this heap of soil at the end of the plot where you propose to finish. If you divide the plot in half down its length, this final strip will be beside the trench which you take out first of all. This means that the soil is moved the minimum distance.

As you move up the first half of the plot remove the top inch or two and put it into the bottom of the trench you have already dug. This top few inches contains the weeds and weed seeds and if you bury them in this way they will not trouble you in the season ahead. The first trench is then filled with the soil which comes out of the next trench and so on along the plot.

Hold the spade upright, as in this way you can get all your weight behind it. You will be able to keep the edges of the trench clean and tidy and the job will run along more easily. If the soil is wet and clinging to the blade of the spade then leave it until the soil is easier to work.

Double digging

This technique is useful when you are preparing a plot for the first time and want to get deeper into the soil; you will dig down to a couple of spits, about 20 inch. *But if your soil has only shallow top soil then don't do it.* Sub-soil is not fertile in most cases and is better left where it is. Double digging established land is generally pointless; remember that nutrients in the soil lie only in the top foot and what goes on below this level is largely irrelevant.

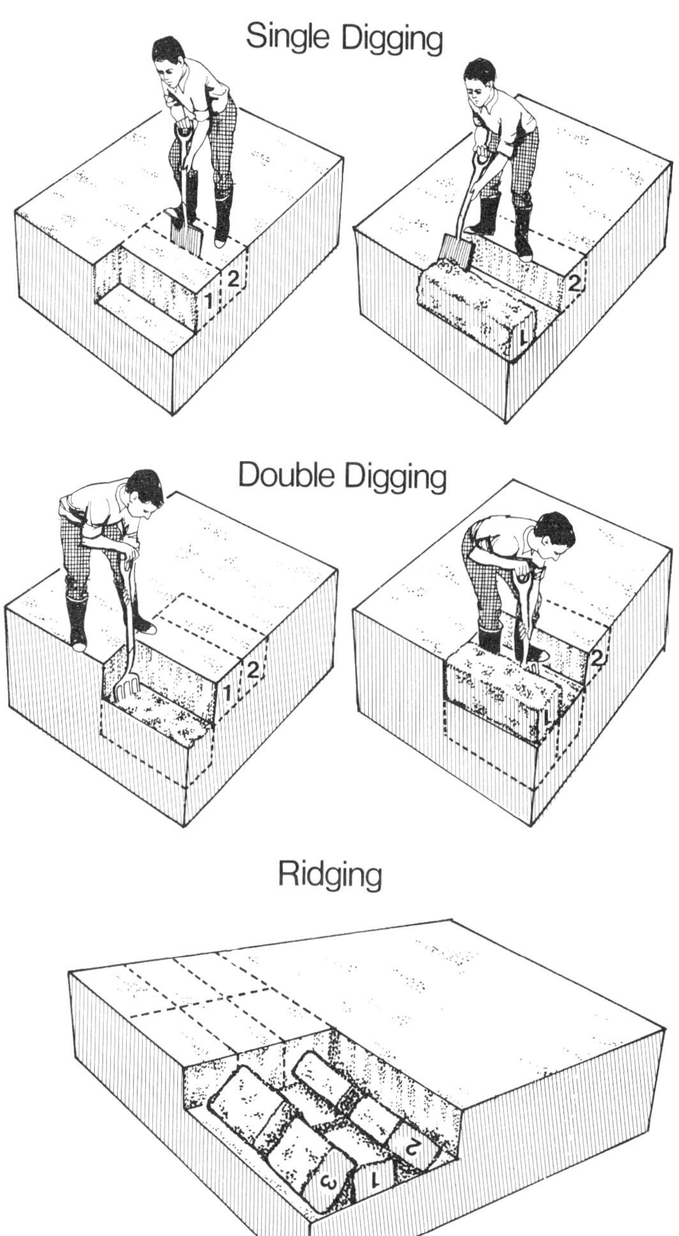
Single Digging
1
2
2
Double Digging
1
2
2
Ridging
3
1
2

When double digging, compost and manure can be worked deep into the soil and this is done once the first trench has been dug and the soil deposited beside the site of the final trench, as with single digging. A wider trench is needed than for single digging, 2 feet as opposed to 6 or 9 inches. When the first spit has been dug out, the bottom spit is forked over and the manure and compost are worked in.

The top soil from the next trench is put onto the forked-over bottom spit in the preceding trench and so on up the plot.

Ridging

A useful technique on very heavy soils as it leaves as much soil as possible exposed to the winter weather. Mark out your plot in rows 2 feet wide and then take out a trench one spit deep at one end of these rows. This earth is taken to the other end of the plot to fill in the final trench. Stand facing your trench and take a spadeful of earth from the middle and move it into the centre of the trench. The left hand spadeful goes alongside it and the right hand spadeful follows it leaving a natural ridge in the centre of the heap. Work your way along the row leaving a rough ridge behind you and then work up the next two feet wide strip.

Final breaking down and forking

With all digging the final breaking down of the soil should be left until the soil is dry in the spring. Then it is a matter of going over the top few inches with a fork and a rake.

Incidentally, if you only want to turn the soil over and you are not considering adding manure or compost then forking can be quite enough. Simply turn the soil over and break up the biggest lumps with the back of the fork as you go along. There is no need for trenching.

Mechanical Cultivation

If this vision of hand labour has depressed you, how about using a mechanical cultivator or rotavator. This is an expensive piece of machinery, but it can either be hired or you can engage a contractor to do the job for you. It is not too expensive.

It will not go as deep as a spade but will churn the soil into fine fragments (and also, unfortunately, perennial weeds, every piece of which will grow again!). Better perhaps for lighter soil than for heavy, which may require rotavating two or three times at intervals when the conditions have to be just right.

20

Make the most of your soil

GORDON COOPER

This subject, I am sure, warrants careful consideration. It may not be a once-for-all matter, like laying the lawn, which if bodged is sometimes impossible to put right without starting again, but, quite obviously, everything in your garden depends on the soil. So, before you plan or plant the garden, find out what your soil is like and, if it is any way inadequate, do what is reasonable to put things right. It is much easier to do this general sort of job all at once—clearing the decks as it were—than to tinker along all the time. Of this we may be sure—it is not enough to buy good plants and put them into the ground. Many plants will put up with this kind of thing and some even thrive on poor soil but many of the best plants need special soil conditions.

What soil consists of

Soil can be a mixture of clay, sand or silt, chalk and humus (broken down vegetable and animal matter) and ideal soil would be a "medium loam" where sand, silt and clay, and humus are in equal proportions. There are few soils so happily balanced but it is the aim of the gardener to get as close to this loam as he can in order to grow the widest possible range of plants.

Sandy soils

Loam lies between sandy soil at one extreme and clay at the other. Pick up a handful of soil. If it has a hard gritty feel even when wet, then it will probably be sandy. A further test is to squeeze it in your hand; if it falls apart when the pressure is released then this again suggests sand. This ability of the soil particles to separate means that the soil will lose moisture quickly and the garden will need plenty of watering during the summer. In addition the soil will not hold the foods that the plant will need to live, so additional feeding will be called for. For this reason sandy soil is often called hungry soil.

There are advantages with sandy soil—drainage will be good and you will be able to work it at all times of the year; sandy soil usually warms up quickly, so that early crops do well.

If your soil is of this type then you must add plenty of humus-making materials to increase the body of the soil and get some "heart" into it. Manure is the first essential and this should be dug in during the winter, along with other bulky organic materials. Humus by itself is not enough—add fertiliser (see p. 149) to the soil just before sowing or planting and again at regular intervals throughout the year.

Clay soils

From one extreme to the other. Clay soil holds water—the soil in your hand will have a slippery feel while the ball you get after squeezing it will certainly not break down into individual crumbs of soil. Clay soils become waterlogged and cold in winter, so early crops are out of the question. Clay dries out slowly in the spring but when it gets really dry the soil hardens up and cracks. Spring digging, therefore, gives the soil little chance to make tilth and autumn digging is essential. On the credit side, however, clay soils are rich in plant foods and once you have improved the texture you will get first rate crops and flowers.

Changing the nature of clay soils can be a lengthy and expensive business. In really bad localities it may be necessary to start by putting drains down (see Lawns p. 193). The next step is to add plenty of compost and manure when digging the soil in the autumn. Do it then and you will find the soil is still workable but leave it until the winter and—oh dear! Another advantage of digging at this time of the year is that you can leave the ground rough and get the frost to work on it for you. A dressing of lime will also help break the clay up but, before adding lime, test the soil to make sure that it will not become too alkaline. The amount to add will depend on the result of the test which can be done very simply, using a soil-testing kit. If your garden will not take lime work $\frac{1}{2}$ lb. of gypsum into the top four inches of each square yard of soil. But insist on horticultural gypsum—raw powdered calcium sulphate.

Chalk soil

Chalk soil is ideal for many plants but it may get sticky in wet weather and can therefore be hard to work during the winter. As a rule water gets away quickly as the top soil can be very shallow and in this case you will have to water during the summer. This fast drainage takes much of the plant food with it, so add plenty of manure or compost when digging the soil over. Do not dig deeply on chalk soil if there is a danger of bringing the sub-soil to the surface. Green manuring is also practised on chalk soils and this consists of growing a fast, inexpensive crop like mustard and then digging it in whilst it is still green.

Stony soil

If you have stony soil then you have problems. Plants don't grow in stones so take off the biggest ones and work as much manure, compost and peat into the top few inches as you can. Stony soils drain well but dry out very quickly. Adding compost will be a continuing business, as the rain tends to wash the nutrients away.

Peaty soil

Just the opposite of stony soil, a heavy peat soil will hold plenty of moisture even to the extent of needing artificial drainage to get rid of some of it. It is dark and spongy in appearance and few gardens are pure peat. Such soil is fertile and, with generous applications of lime, will grow good plants. Peat soils do however vary and before adding lime make sure that your soil needs it.

Testing your soil

On any garden soil it is important to know about the degree of acidity or alkalinity that you enjoy. This is known as the pH reading and while pH7 is neutral, figures above this on the scale denote alkalinity and below pH7 the degree of acidity. With the Murphy Analoam tester which costs a few shillings you can test your soil by making a solution of soil and water, then add a tablet. The colour of the solution is then checked against a scale and

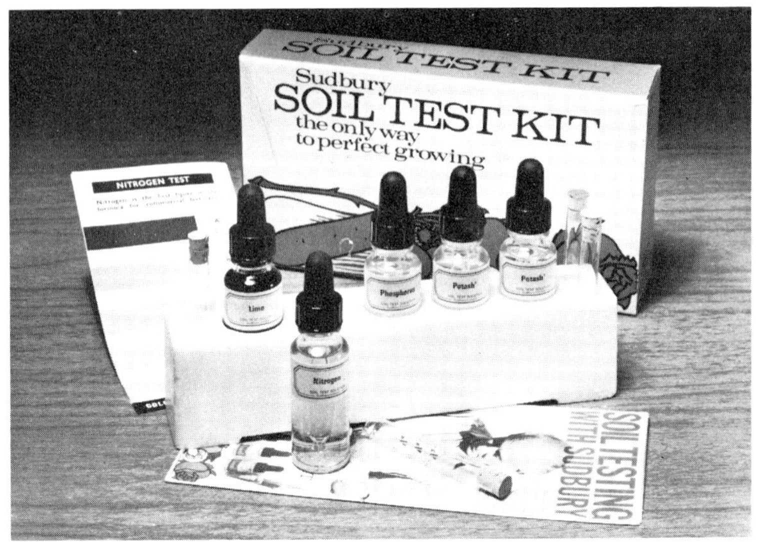

A soil testing kit.

according to the colour reading you can take the appropriate action.

For more comprehensive information about the nature of your soil the Sudbury Soil Test Kit is invaluable. As well as pH it will tell you if your soil is deficient in the Nitrogen, Phosphorus and Potash which are the main plant foods that your soil must provide if the plants are to thrive. In addition the Sudbury Kit tells you how much of which fertiliser you will need to bring the soil to optimum condition.

The use of peat

Now let us turn to the various things we can add to the soil, starting with peat. This is an entirely natural commodity, the product of years of laying down of all sorts of vegetation. It has been described as a sort of huge compost heap built by nature. There are several different peats but the similarities are more important than the differences and some suppliers offer an all-purpose product.

For general soil improvement peat is worked into the top few inches of the soil before sowing or planting. This helps to hold moisture, while the plant is establishing itself, and also supplies humus. When preparing the ground for lawn construction a generous application worked into the top six inches will get the seed away to a good start and give extra springiness to the finished lawn. Peat is most widely used as a mulch—a layer of organic material over wet soil to keep in the moisture. Mulching also discourages weed growth, looks attractive and eventually helps the soil structure when it is dug in at the end of the year.

A common mistake when applying peat mulch is to apply it to dry soil. The peat makes it harder for the rain and any artificial watering to get through to the soil. Even worse is to put peat on when the peat itself is dry, for it may well absorb moisture from the soil, thus drying the plant out even more. Dry peat absorbs an enormous amount of water and is difficult to wet once it has dried. It must be soaking when it is applied if it is to do any good.

Peat in its dry state is a good insulator and can be used to protect over-wintering bulbs. When planting outside, a handful around the bulb helps.

The use of lime

Most gardens need some lime. Without it, the soil turns sour; once this happens the bacteria and the worms suffer and in a short time the plants follow suit. We have already considered lime as a soil conditioner for clay soils; it is also an essential plant food, providing calcium and, by its action on humus, other plant foods. It discourages slugs, leatherjackets and wireworms, and club root which affects cabbages and cauliflowers.

Hydrated lime is the grade to use although ground chalk is also effective. If your soil is sandy or a light loam, then a normal application would be 8 oz. to the square yard, while on heavy soils this should increase to $\frac{3}{4}$ lb. per square yard. There is no need to dig lime in, for the rain will wash it in for you quickly enough.

The use of fertilisers

There are two sorts of chemicals that plants need for healthy growth: the main plant foods nitrogen, phosphate and potash, and minor or "trace" elements, iron, sulphur, boron, copper and one or two others.

Nitrogen promotes good leaf growth so foliage plants and

grass show signs of any nitrogen shortage very quickly—pale colour and small leaves. Phosphates are needed for good root formation and, if your plants look stunted and have only minimal root structures, look out for phosphate shortage. Potash makes flowers colourful, and fruit and vegetables tasty. A shortage is sometimes indicated by leaves scorching at the edges and poor flowers.

Fertilisers are described as either "organic", if they are of animal or vegetable origin, or "inorganic", if they are manufactured or artificially made. For nitrogen, use sulphate of ammonia (inorganic) at 1 oz. to the square yard, or dried blood (organic) at 1½ oz. to the square yard. For phosphates apply superphosphate of lime (inorganic) at 2–3 oz. per square yard or bonemeal (organic) at 3–4 oz. per square yard. Potash is provided by sulphate of potash (inorganic) at 1½ oz. per square yard or wood ashes (organic) at 8 oz. per square yard. Do not apply sulphate of ammonia after mid season as it encourages soft growth, which is vulnerable to winter damage. John Innes Base Fertiliser provides a balanced year-round fertiliser and many gardeners use it in this way as well as in John Innes Compost. Fertilisers of this type should be worked into the top few inches of the soil while the plants are growing, as in this way they can get straight to the roots of the plants where they are needed. Bonemeal and hoofs and horn are slow in action and are useful for giving a boost to long living plants that require nourishment over a period of time.

There is a school of thought that suggests that constant application of inorganic fertilisers has a depressing effect on the soil and can harm the humus content, but there is no concrete evidence to support this. It is, however, advisable to ensure regular applications of compost, peat and well rotted manure to keep the soil well supplied with humus. Moreover, humus provides the trace elements that make up the right feeding mix.

Three further points: firstly, as many fertilisers are available in compound packs with the nitrogen, phosphates and potash blended to suit the needs of particular plants, it is important to follow the maker's instructions. Some of the amounts may seem very small but over-generous dosage can do more harm than good. Secondly, when applying fertilisers keep them off foliage as they can scorch the leaves. If you are applying the fertiliser during a dry spell it may pay you, therefore, to *water* it into the soil. Thirdly, plants want fertilisers in the top few inches of the soil so there is no point in really digging them in. Slow acting bone-meal *can* be dug into the soil during the winter digging but not more than about nine inches deep. The fast acting types are best raked or hoed into the top few inches.

The need for humus

The vital element in the soil structure. This decomposed animal and vegetable material is the stuff which the bacteria breaks down. It feeds and supports these millions of microscopic organisms that keep soil healthy. Every crop you take out of the garden reduces the organic content and this content must be put back. For this reason the compost heap is an important part of the successful gardening cycle

21

How to plan and stock a garden

GORDON COOPER

A garden can have many purposes, even to the extent that it doesn't even have to be a *horticultural* purpose. It can just be an area of land, kept clear of weeds for the neighbour's sake, by the most brutal of methods, such as a scythe—whoops, mind your feet! This you can use for kids' football or sun-lounging.

But generally it is used for some horticulture and, if you are to plan it properly, it is important that you know clearly what you want your garden for. It may be the challenge of growing plants that other people have trouble with. You may grow plants simply to have cut flowers for the house. Perhaps you want lots of vegetables and fruit to help in keeping down the cost of living and for the pleasure of fresh produce. Perhaps you want to keep up with the Jones's, or simply to have a nice tidy plot in which you can sit on a summer evening knowing that the work you have done has increased the value of your property.

What follows are the factors involved in completing any plan. I can't tell you how to plan it, for only you know what you want and what you have already got.

Outside help

Not to be ignored. Many nursery firms have landscape garden departments and they will send an expert along to look at your site and discuss ideas with you. A plan is prepared and an estimate supplied to cover the work to be done and the plants that will be needed. In most cases a charge is made for the visit and the plan, to cover the expenses incurred, but this need not be expensive and it does ensure that with this expert advice you will get a wide range of plants and a realistic layout. Most gardeners have only a limited experience of plants while the nurseryman makes his living from them, and this will show in the varieties he suggests. This can include your own favourites but it will pay you to go along with the nurseryman's suggestions and recommendations.

Laying out the garden

Whether your garden is completely new or an updating of someone else's efforts there are some basic guide lines. These are of particular importance in a small plot as there is not much room to spare and mistakes in initial planning can be difficult to hide. If the garden you inherited on moving house is a neglected wilderness, approach the redesigning of it as though you were starting from the beginning.

First of all make a plan on graph paper on which you indicate the shape of the plot, its dimensions, aspects and any fixed features that you are unlikely to move. By this I mean large trees, manhole covers, existing concrete paths that you do not want to take out and so on. These are features that have to be designed around but they need not necessarily be drawbacks to an attractive design. The tree can accommodate climbing plants and naturalised bulbs, the manhole cover can be hidden by careful planting while the paths can be cleaned up and modified to look pleasant.

On this paper plan you can mark out the respective areas for the flowers, fruit and vegetables, extra paths that have to be laid, where the greenhouse is to go; by planning this way you can do the construction work in the right order. There is little point in putting down concrete paths and then finding that laying the electricity cable for the greenhouse will mean digging the path up again.

I mentioned aspect as one of the items to be marked on the plan. While you are deciding which *is* north, have a look at the tall features on surrounding properties. Are they likely to block the sun from what might otherwise be a promising area for a flower bed.

Do not omit the areas for storing stakes, soils and other bits and pieces. This should be the least promising area from a

A grid plan and what it would look like from your back window.

cultivation point of view and allow sufficient space for a compost heap, a garden shed and for a bonfire. The greenhouse, by the way, is not likely to do best at this same spot and, if you can find a sunny area close to the house, its running will be simplified. It will be easier and cheaper to lay on electricity and water, and you will not have long walks down the garden on cold winter nights.

I discuss soil testing on page 147 and the question of drainage on page 193 and it is important that you should attend to these points before going any further. If you are going to be involved in major drainage then the time to do it is at this preliminary stage and not when half the garden has been laid out (see the chapter on Lawns).

Site levelling can be undertaken either over the whole area or on smaller parts of it, but it must be done with care. In most gardens it is neither necessary nor, in my view, desirable. Irregular slopes can be a great asset and can be utilised to create interesting effects. If you decide to do some levelling then look after your most precious asset, the top soil, by removing it first and then level up by moving the sub soil. (And my goodness, if that doesn't put you off unnecessary levelling, I don't know what will!) Once you have achieved the desired level then put the top soil back. be particularly careful about levelling on heavy clay soil or you may lose the natural drainage and create waterlogged areas.

Flower beds and borders. Try to avoid straight lines. The back of the border may well run against a straight fence or path but the front should be curved so that areas cut out into the lawn. You will then find that you cannot see all of the border at a glance and this makes the garden look larger. *Hide* some of the garden by the shape of the borders and the heights of the plants you put on these promontories. A standard tree in this sort of location looks really splendid. Don't make the beds too narrow. Five foot is a good minimum—wide enough to carry a good selection of plants of varying heights and yet not too wide for you to get at the soil with a hoe.

When actually marking out the border on the site use a guide to make sure that you are following the shapes that you have designed. A garden hose laid on the ground and held in place with a few wooden pegs works very well and it is also long enough for you to visualise the cultivated area before driving the spade into the soil.

Paths. First of all, think what a path is for. Are you sure you need them? I often feel that the most useful paths are those in larger flower beds, to enable you to husband them without getting mucky. A flat path round the garden does enable you to walk round in light shoes when the grass is wet but how often are you going to want to do it? Is it such an inconvenience to change into heavier shoes, so that you can walk on the grass?

Now don't misunderstand me, I am not "against" paths. What I am against is paths that are not part of a plan, that are not thought through. If you have a path, make it interesting, make it a feature of the garden, make it lead the eye up the garden, make it purposeful. Don't just put it there because you think all gardens have paths. What's wrong with a grass path, after all. If you have heavy traffic along them you can always sink paving slabs just below grass level and at convenient stepping distance. (Incidentally, make them wide enough for your mower to move along.)

A note on rockeries

A rockery must not look like a dog's graveyard, with little stones sticking forlornly up. A rockery should appear as though it is a *natural* outcrop of rock, such as you see on moorland. Thus sloping land is generally the only suitable setting if the garden is small (if large you can make your own artificial slopes with a rockery integrated into them). The rocks should be large—24 inches by 12 inches is the sort of size—and laid as though part of the natural rock strata. The rocks ought to blend into the natural environment so, if you are on sloping land where there is some rock, you must buy those of similar appearance.

The above may read rather discouragingly, but the fact is that most "rockeries" look awful. They are often started because of a desire to grow the small plants associated with them but remember that such plants can be grown by other methods—in a dry-stone wall, for example. Moreover, when you consider that a well tended rockery plant will grow so that it smothers your expensive stones, I think you may agree with me that a dry stone wall is better.

If your garden is large or sloped and if you can afford the large rocks required and if you can manage to hump them into position, then I believe you can make a fine feature. It could,

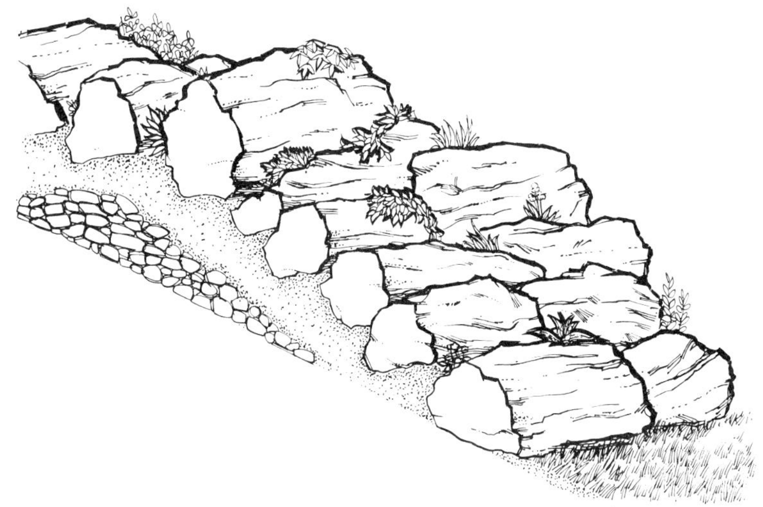

A well-built rockery reproduces the natural look of an outcrop of stone. Strata lines must be horizontal and the stones must be laid in layers.

indeed, be superb, if combined with a pond or waterfall as described by Mike Smith in Chapter 18. If, however, you lack these features, and if you want to grow rockery plants, my advice is to go for the dry stone wall.

Planning for planting

Having completed the grand plan, built the paths, prepared the beds, the next step is buying the plants, seeds, bulbs and trees to complete the picture within its frame.

Never judge a plant by its price. Comparisons are difficult as you cannot relate plants grown by different nurseries unless you have a look at them and know something about the factors that determine relative quality. This calls for some experience and a lot of free time, which most of us do not have. The best advice is still to rely on a reputable nursery or a reliable mail order company that has a reputation it is proud of and wishes to maintain.

This is not to say that even the best nurseries do not have occasional complaints. Postal traffic is always open to trouble and if plants are delayed in transit they can suffer severe damage.

A dry stone wall is the ideal place for planting alpines and other small perennial plants. Such walls are made up stones without any mortar, laid in rows and sloping slightly inwards to capture the rain. Reconstituted stones can be bought from garden centres and are ideal for the purpose. Soil is packed tightly between the walls.

But the good nursery will endeavour to replace plants that reach you in poor condition, provided you advise them quickly if this appears to be the case. You cannot expect much sympathy if you complain after the plants have been in your garden several months and then die. Let the nursery know right away, within a few days of delivery.

If you concentrate on raising a particular type of plant you may well deal with a specialist nursery. Over the years they will be able to advise you in building up your collection and a very pleasant relationship can develop when you visit their nurseries or talk to the company's staff at the big shows like Chelsea, Southport and Shrewsbury.

Always buy good stock, whether it is seed, bulbs, shrubs or anything else. The amount of work involved is much greater if you are trying to keep poor plants alive and the effect is always a disappointment when compared to what might have been.

Gardening catalogues contain a wealth of invaluable information. Descriptions, colour pictures, cultural instructions are all there and particular advice about planting distances, spread and height of plants, flowering times and all the other details which help you to plan your garden and make it look the way it should. Most of them are free but some nurseries make a nominal charge for the more ambitious catalogues, though they are still good value for money. What plants to choose? Take my advice and choose the plants you like the look of. You'll soon find out how to grow them and, even if you fail, what does it matter? Remember, there are absolutely hundreds of plants!

"Instant" gardening

This is one of the catch phrases which the purists loath, but the fact is that the development of container-grown and containerised plants has meant that you can call in at your Garden Centre and take away with you the plants you want, growing in cans or plastic containers. These are taken off when you get home and the plant put straight into the ground at any time of the year, without any set back.

The advantages are obvious: you can plant up an entire bed or border over the weekend but if you want to leave it for a week or two then, as long as you remember to keep the plants watered, they will continue to thrive. Furthermore, you can pick the individual plant you like from a group of plants of the variety in question without even knowing its name!

On the other side of the coin, some plants grow better than others in containers and, unless you know how long the plant has been growing in its container, you can be unlucky. A shrub which has spent all its growing life in the same container will have a root ball carrying plenty of soil, so that the transplanting operation will not do any harm, provided it is planted in the garden with the soil at the same level as in the container. However, for the plant that has only just been containerised, transplanting can be a real shock as the soil will tend to fall away when the container is removed and it will have to try and re-settle all over again. Guard also, incidentally, against a tendency to take a plant in flower from the nursery because it looks attractive, even though there is no place for it in your original planting plan. (Which you have very clearly in your mind, of course!)

Bare root stock

Of course, the traditional method of buying plants continues to operate, with selected plants coming to you in the spring and autumn at their correct planting times. These plants are referred to for convenience as "bare root" and as they do not have a root surrounded by soil in most cases, they need to be planted right away. In particular this applies to shrubs, trees and roses sent through the post. They will frequently need a good soaking before planting because of the moisture loss in transit. These should be first class plants as long as they have been purchased from a reputable nursery, and many specialised plants can only be obtained in this way as your Garden Centre will probably not stock them.

A note on planting

There is nothing mysterious about what is needed for successful planting and transplanting. If newly bedded plants fail it is fundamentaly due to one reason—you have not protected them against the jolting shock of being lifted out of one bed, where the roots were nicely taking up moisture and food, and put into another, where the tiny root fibres have to search out anew the required sources of nutriment—and have to search them out quickly. That once understood, what to do becomes quite clear.

The general strictures about soil in Chapter 20 must be even more carefully adhered to, i.e. the soil that the root fibres are to meet needs to be well-balanced in general but just a little richer than normal—that means added humus and a little extra fertiliser. The roots must be preserved with the fibres on—these act as emergency feeders while the plant urgently puts out new root fibres. The soil must be fine enough for the fibres to make contact—great voids of air between big clods will feed nothing. The roots must be prevented from moving, so the soil must be packed well into them and then firmed well down. The purpose of a stake is not so much to keep a plant upright, but rather to stop the roots from moving in the ground and so losing close contact with the soil.

That is really all there is to it. Now, of course, some plants withstand shock better than others and so very many books have been compiled on detailed care. Buy these if you want to make sure of a plant, but in general the above should suffice.

What about the correct time for planting? Well, I think you can see that if you plant when nature is dormant, i.e. not in blazing mid-summer, a plant has less shock to withstand. Therefore early spring and late autumn are the best. Mid-winter is all right except for evergreens and particularly conifers but . . . ugh! However, you *can* plant at any time—the chances of plants surviving the shock obviously varies, but there is always a chance. And obviously container plants (see p. 123) help here enormously.

Plants for special purposes

As you look over the site when planning your own garden you will find that there are areas of trouble. Hot dry spots, damp areas, steep banks with shallow top soil, stony areas, shaded areas. You may need plants that marauding rabbits will not dine off or perhaps the idea of winter colour appeals to you. All these requirements can be met so let us have a look at some of the most popular plants in these various categories.

Plants for ground cover. This can be the labour saving part of gardening as one of the most back breaking jobs in the garden is getting rid of weeds. It can be done chemically or by hand, but better than either is the planting of selected plants to cover the ground and smother weed growth. It will be a year or two after planting before the plants are big enough to form this protective mat but at least you are making a start.

Perennial plants to use for ground cover include Bergenia (megasea), Ericas (heathers), Lamium galeobdolon variegatum, Geraniums (not pelargoniums), Anaphalis, Saponaria ocymoides and Hostas, while among the hardy shrubs are Veronica pageana and Veronica buxifolia, Pachysandra and Hypericum. By nature these plants are on the short side, hardy and interesting because of their flower or their foliage and in some cases both.

Shrubs for shade under trees. Aucuba, Azalea, Berberis, Broom, Cotoneaster, Laurustinus, Olearia, Pachysandra, Rhododendrons, Ribes, Daphne, Hypericum, Skimmia, Viburnum.

Perennials for shady areas. Acanthus spinosus, Anaphalis, Campanula muralis, Epimedium, Geranium, Lamium, Iris foetidissima, Omphalodes, Pulmonaria, Tiarella, Vinca.

Shrubs for dry banks. Berberis aquifolium, Cistus, Cotoneaster, Broom, Lonicera nitida, Olearia, Phlomis, Potentilla, Rhus cotinus, Ribes, Fuchsia, Heather, Hypericum, Lavender, Santolina, Spirea, Tamarix, Veronica.

Shrubs that rabbits leave alone. Azalea, Berberis, Laurustinus, Rhododendron, Cornus, Fuchsia, Hawthorn, Spirea, Viburnum.

Shrubs for winter flowering. Daphne Mezereum, Hamamellis, Heather, Mahonia Bealei, Rhododendron praecox, Viburnum fragrans.

Evergreen shrubs to grow in chalky soil. Aucuba, Ceanothus, Cedrus Atlantica, Choisya, Cistus, Cotoneaster, Juniper, Osmanthus, Photinia, Privet, Cupressus macrocarpa, Escallonia, Gorse, Pyracantha, Spartium, Veronica, Yucca, Yew.

Plants for wet areas and beside ponds. Astrantia, Astilbe, Caltha, Gentiana asclepiadea, Iris sibirica, Iris kaempferi, Lythrum, Monarda, Polygonum, Senecio, Trollius.

Shrubs for wet areas· Cornus alba, Hippophae, Leycesteria, Populus, Ribes, Salix, Spiraea, Thuya, Viburnum opulus.

Shrubs for acid soils. Rhododendron, Heaths and Heathers, Camellias, Kalmia latifolia, Azaleas.

Shrubs for alkaline soils. Most plants except those that need acid soils (above) grow well in alkaline soils provided that the condition is not severe when steps should be taken to rectify it.

Shrubs for winter colour. Chimonanthus, Cornus mas, Hamamellis, Jasminum nudiflorum, Lonicera purpusii, Mahonia, Sycopsis, Viburnum bodnantense, Viburnum fragrans, Daphne mezereum.

Plants for town gardens. Don't worry too much about this. The air is much cleaner than it used to be in most town areas. As a general rule avoid evergreens, though even they can be O.K. if sprayed with clean water to remove the dirt.

Plants for Camouflage

Perhaps it is an unsightly object such as a garden shed or oil storage tank that you wish to camouflage. The Russian Vine (Polygonum baldschuanicum) is the standby usually recommended. There are other plants, in addition to those already mentioned. The climbing Hydrangea (Hydrangea petiolaris), Forsythia suspensa, Celastrus and Vitis coignetiae will cover an eyesore.

Plants for a Wall

For a south or westerly aspect the choice is wide; it is when you want something to grow against a wall facing north or east that your problems begin. What will grow?

Ironclad shrubs are the Firethorns (Pyracantha): P. atlantioides, and P. crenulata rogersiana, both bearing crimson berries; the Japanese Quince (Chaenomeles), familiarly known as "japonica". Red currant is also a practical proposition.

Climbing roses flourish surprisingly, e.g. "Handel", "Golden Showers", "Etude", "Félicité et Perpétue", "Allen Chandler", climbing "Caroline Tertout" and "Dr. Van Fleet". Remember, these plants are not self supporting and will need to be tied to a galvanised nail driven into the wall.

Two species of honeysuckle demand almost complete shade: Lonicera tellmanniana and L. tragophylla, both having large flowers. Clematis: on a bitterly cold wall I have grown C. flammula which produced masses of scented flowers in the autumn. These are twining plants and will need a trellis or a strip of wide mesh wire netting.

Ivy is not to be condemned. Clinging close with its tiny sucker-like roots it will not harm your house as generally supposed. Quite the opposite, it will keep the brickwork dry and free from atmospheric corrosion. Do make sure, though, that the brickwork and pointing is sound to start with. Then plant the golden foliaged Ivy. (Hedera helix "Buttercup"). Ivy must be maintained. Every spring clip all the leaves away and trim back shoots that are getting too close to paintwork, windows and gutters. Never let it get beyond your reach.

Plant names

Why are plants named as they are? Why are there sometimes so many words. The reason is to avoid confusion in what is, after all, an international subject. Latin and Greek has been adopted as the basis for plant naming since these are universal, ancient languages. It is a good system for the layman gardener even if he does not boast a latin education, for by understanding a few key words he can have a fair idea of the appearance or habit of the plant—just from its name. There are several little books about such names.

Most plants have more than one word to their name; each word is a progressive refinement of the description. Thus the first name is the generic name generally the "name" as we know it. E.g. Laburnum. This generic name can have various origins. Often it will be the name of the botanist connected with the plant, e.g. the Dahlia is named after the Swedish botanist Andreas Dahl, the Buddleia takes its name from an English botanist and parson, Adam Buddle. Both of these botanists were comparative newcomers to having plants named after them, even though both are eighteenth century characters! How about Helenium named after Helen of Troy or Achillea named after Achilles, the famous Greek warrior. Names of people and families often occur later in the description, e.g. *Potentilla fruticosa vilmoriniana*. The name indicates that it is a potentilla, that is shrubby (fruticosa) and that this particular variety was developed by the famous Vilmorin family, which has been prominent in horticulture since the mid nineteenth century and is still active in France today. Similarly *Sinensis*—from China; *Kewensis*—from Kew.

22

Propagating

GORDON COOPER

This is the do-it-yourself part of growing your own plants, instead of going out and buying them. It is not difficult as long as you observe a few basic rules and the satisfaction is immense. It is the best part of gardening—what it's all about really. Whether you increase your plant stock by division, cuttings, layering, splitting up bulbs or sowing seeds this is one part of gardening that does not involve hard physical work. A gardener who is particularly successful in propagating may be accused of having "green fingers" but it is usually not so much a matter of luck as of taking care.

Growing from seed

This is by far the most common propagation method. The degree of success enjoyed will vary according to the nature of the seed and the way it is treated. Every seed is a plant in miniature with a supply of food inside its case. Our aim is to encourage the seed to develop and the first requirement is water, which is absorbed into the seed. A little warmth and the seed starts to grow until eventually it breaks through the casing and puts out a root system and a stem. The third basic requirement to get the plant started is air, and this is why an open soil structure is important. Once it has begun to grow the seed will need additional food and we must provide this in the soil in such a form that the plant can reach it and use it. For this reason the soil structure must be a fine granular one in which the little roots can make contact with the granules.

Seed can be grown both in the open ground and under cover. By this I mean grown in a seed box in the house or in the greenhouse with a cover to prevent excessive moisture loss at this critical stage of seed growth.

Only "hardy" seeds will grow in the garden and this is why spring is the best time to plant them. The soil is getting warm after the winter, the right amount of moisture is present and there will be plenty of rain to come before the dryness of summer.

Many varieties of plants are willing to start their seeds into growth in the autumn, immediately after flowering themselves, but these plants will not be hardy enough to stand the winter so there is little point in allowing this to happen. It is better to start them off under protection, either early in the spring or late in the winter and these plants are called "half hardy" for obvious reasons. Let us look at the various sorts of plants in more detail.

Hardy Annuals (H.A.)

These plants are sown, grow, flower and die in one year. They are hardy in that they live all their lives out of doors in our climate and include Alyssum, Calendula, Larkspur, Mignonette, Nasturtium, Sunflowers and Virginia Stock among many others. They are generally sown in the open ground between the end of March and the end of April but suffer little delay in flowering if the sowing is left over for a few days.

Prepare the soil carefully to make a fine seed bed. After general soil preparation, wait for a day when the soil is dry on the surface and then firm the soil down well and rake it over to make a light crumb structure. This is most important as small seeds get lost in heavy lumpy soil. Time spent on the soil at this stage is time well spent.

Once the seed bed is ready the seed can be sown broadcast or in drills. If you are preparing a border of annual flowers, mark out on the seed bed the areas that each variety is to occupy, sow the seeds inside these areas as thinly as possible and then lightly rake over. With very small seed it helps to mix the seed with a little sand as it can then be handled more easily. Water the bed well and unless you have a dry spell when more watering will be needed, this is all that is needed until germination takes place.

Once the seedlings have developed a pair of leaves and they are large enough to handle they will need to be thinned out.

Even allowing for the fact that many seeds will fail to germinate, they will nevertheless grow so thickly that few will survive the competition for space, moisture and food so thin them out according to variety. Calendula, for example will need 12 inches between each plant while smaller plants like Alyssum need only 6 inches. (For vegetables, see p. 211).

Half Hardy Annuals (H.H.A.)

Like hardy annuals these plants work through their life cycle in one year but they are too tender to stand up to any frost so they are sown under glass and transplanted into the open garden once they have been hardened off and all danger of frost is passed.

The seed is sown either in seed boxes or shallow pans, depending upon the number of plants you propose to raise. The first thing to go into the container is a layer of broken crocks over the drainage holes. To try and raise seed in containers without drainage holes in the base is invariably unsuccessful, but put the crocks in and a layer of leaf mould or peat over the crocks to stop the compost being washed away when watering. I mention compost, as soil straight out of the garden is unsatisfactory—it is full of weed seeds and short in plant foods. The correct grade of proprietary compost is a careful blend designed to get the seed off to a good start.

Some gardeners like to mix up their own composts but the John Innes range made up by a reliable supplier will contain just the right amounts of loam, peat, sand, superphosphate of lime and chalk. If you want to cut down on the available range of composts then the Levington range is a good alternative. Here only two grades are offered, one for sowing and one for potting but they are certainly successful.

Slightly overfill the seed box with compost and then scrape off the surplus; firm down, particularly in the corners, so that the soil level is about half an inch below the rim of the box. The compost must be watered before the seed is sown and this is best done by lowering the box into a tray of water which is shallow enough to prevent the water rising over the sides of the box. The compost will absorb water from below by capillary action; as soon as the surface starts to turn dark you will know that the water has risen through.

Sow thinly, and cover the seed with a light application of

compost or even sand. With larger seed and pelleted seed there is no need to sow broadcast as each can be placed on the compost and in this way reduce the need for thinning out. Before covering the boxes, add a label on top of the compost giving the name of the variety and the date when it was sown. Any other information can be added at this stage if you want to check on germination, purity, etc.

Cover the box with a sheet of glass or slide it into a polythene bag as this will keep the moisture in the compost. Germination is also improved if the box is covered and the compost kept in darkness, so a sheet of brown paper over the glass is the final touch.

From now on the boxes must be examined daily. In the first place this will be only to wipe off the condensation which forms on the underside of the glass. As soon as the seedlings break through the soil the brown paper is removed to give them as much light as possible. This must not be direct hot sunshine as this will tend to burn them off.

Pricking out is the next stage in the growth of half hardy plants, for unless you have been able to position the seeds at suitable intervals they will be growing closely together and they must be given more elbow room.

Start pricking out just as soon as the seedlings are large enough to handle and this means just as soon as the first pair of true leaves are in evidence, i.e. not the seed leaves, which appear first. Always handle a seedling by this pair of leaves and not by the stem as any damage here will soon kill it.

Lift out a bunch of seedlings with a small spoon or dibber, worked under the soil so that they are removed without damage to the roots. Then gently separate the seedlings and replant them in another seed box in which you will have crocks and peat plus John Innes Compost No. 1 instead of the John Innes Seed Compost in which the seed was sown. This pricking out is a delicate operation calling for patience. You will need a small tool or pointed stick to make a hole big enough to take the roots of the seedling in comfort. Lower it into this hole and gently work the compost around the roots. Then firm down. Plant the seedlings in rows at about 48 to the box and then water with Cheshunt Compound.

Seedlings at this stage of growth are liable to attack by a number

Transplant seedlings once they are large enough to handle. Hold them by the leaves not the stem. These could have been moved several days earlier.

of fungal diseases, which cause "damping off". The stem seems to collapse and a whole box of plants can be lost in 24 hours. Poor air circulation is a contributory factor. Watering with Cheshunt Compound helps in the fight against this particular trouble.

The seedlings will grow happily now as long as they get plenty of light and water as required. Once they have filled out the box they should be transferred complete into the cold frame (see p. 120) for hardening off prior to planting out in the open garden.

In the frame they will have the benefit of open air during the day and the protection of glass during the cold nights. Once the danger of late frost has passed, the plants are taken out of the seed boxes and planted in the positions where they are to flower in the open garden. It is well worth giving the plants an extra drink of water before this transplanting, so that they suffer as little set-back as possible.

Hardy Perennials (H.P.)

These are plants which flower year after year. In many cases they can be raised from seed and subsequently propagated by division of the roots, like the rest of the perennial family. They can be sown in a spare part of the open garden in a nursery bed prepared like the annual seed bed (see p. 166). Sow in May or June and then transplant them into the positions where they are to flower in the autumn. In most cases they will start their flowering life the following year, but some varieties take a little longer and for Leucojum it may be as long as 3 years. Other perennials like primulus and meconopsis can be sown in the winter and kept in a cold frame until the spring.

Half Hardy Perennials (**H.H.P.**)

Although the ultimate growth pattern is the same as the hardy perennials these varieties must be started under glass until large enough to go outside. Varieties in this group include Arctotis, Lobelia Cardinalis and Eccremocarpus.

Hardy Biennials (**H.B.**)

These plants need two years to complete their growth cycle. Seed is sown in the open garden in May or June and the plant transplanted to its flowering position in the autumn. It will flower in the following spring and is then discarded. Wallflowers, Sweet Williams, Canterbury Bells and Myosotis (Forget-Me-Nots) are all biennials and as such, ideal for spring bedding.

These groups form the greater part of the various types of plants grown from seed but you will also come across other abbreviations.

G.A. Greenhouse Annual. This plant will have a one year growth cycle under glass.

G.B. Greenhouse Biennial. Sow one year and flower the next under glass.

G.P. Greenhouse Perennial. Flower year after year under glass.

G.S. Greenhouse Shrub. Grown from seed this plant will have a normal shrub habit under glass.

F1 Hybrid. Most plants are pollinated casually by insects in the open air and for this reason it is sometimes impossible to be sure about parentage. Seedsmen are constantly trying to improve the qualities of existing varieties and this blending of characteristics is called hybridising. To do it successfully, plants are raised in enclosed environments where pollination is carefully controlled.

In this way the size of one vegetable can be blended with the flavour of another or the colour of one rose with the disease resistance of another. This is not "hit and miss" and calls for a lot of skill together with a certain amount of luck. The first generation of such a cross is called an F1 Hybrid while the second generation is an F2 Hybrid and so on. It does not follow that the strain improves as the generations continue with cross pollination. The original successful cross has to be repeated every year under controlled conditions to make another crop of F1 and F2 seed. For this reason it is not worth collecting the seed from your hybrid plants as they will not come true. It also explains why hybrid seed is more expensive.

Propagation by cuttings

When growing new plants from cuttings the aim is to cut a piece of the plant in question and encourage it to put out roots and start a new life on its own. This is done by taking the right part of the plant at the right time of the year and providing conditions of soil and atmosphere in which it will have the best chance of succeeding.

Not all plants will grow from cuttings—flowers cut in the garden for indoor display continue to grow and the flowers will open further but they will not attempt to put out roots. In the main it is the plants with harder stems that can be propagated in this way—plants like carnations, hydrangeas, roses, clematis, lonicera, camellias ericas and so on.

"Irishman's cuttings" by the way, are shoots taken from a plant, usually from the root, which already have some root structure of their own and we are not really concerned with this. It can work very well, of course, as the plant is already half way there.

There are basically three types of cutting, although they are described in a number of different ways. There are, however, some basic rules that apply to all of them. The soil mixture in which the cuttings are inserted must contain some sand to provide good drainage, as waterlogged soil will kill the cuttings off very

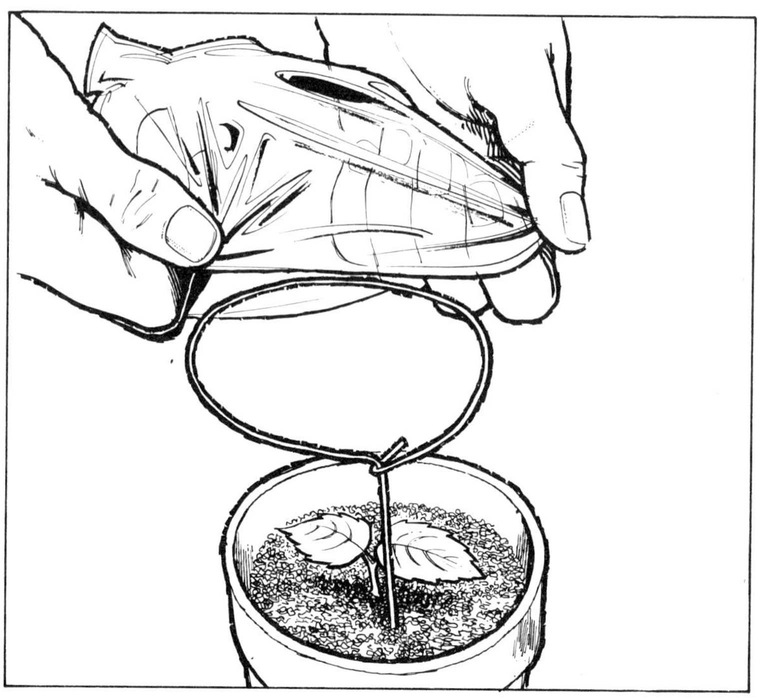

A simple moisture retaining unit is made by draping a polythene bag over a wire shape to hold the bag clear of the plant. Tuck the ends of the bag under the base of the pot.

quickly. Some peat is also useful as cuttings do better in soil that is slightly acid. There must be plant foods and trace elements in the right amounts: a good blend is equal parts of sand, peat and loam. The use of a hormone rooting powder also assists. The final rule is to keep the air moist around the cutting: if you have a special propagating frame then this is no problem but if not then a polythene bag supported by a light wire frame will do admirably. This makes a miniature greenhouse and enables you to take cuttings with a minimum of equipment and space. The kitchen windowsill can be your plant nursery.

Hard-wood cuttings

Sometimes called "ripe cuttings" these are pieces of mature stem with firm bark on them; they are usually taken in the autumn.

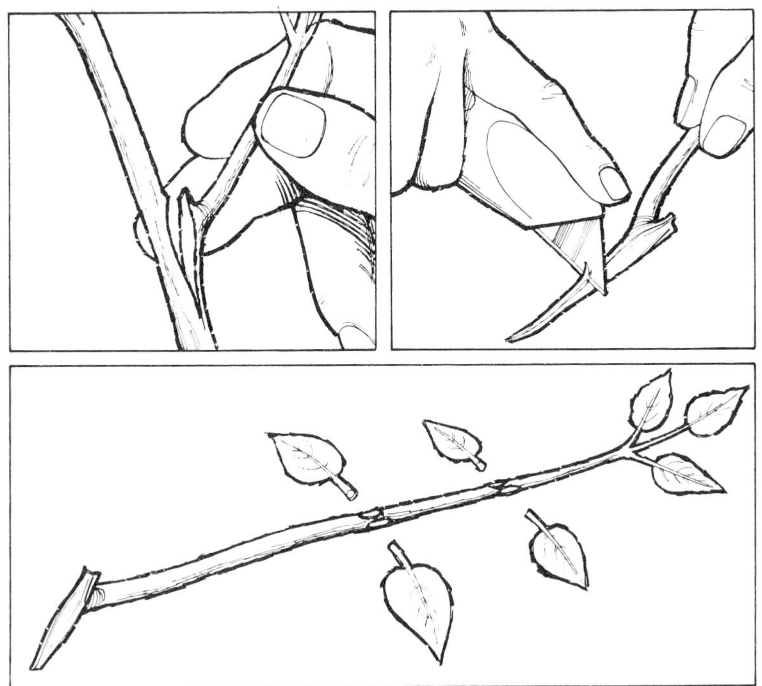

A hard wood cutting ready to insert into John Innes compost.

Select a shoot and take it off the tree with a piece of the main stem on it. This is really a matter of a gentle downward pull. The piece of the main stem is called a "heel". This heel should then be trimmed with a very sharp knife to make clean ends. The final cutting should be 8 or 9 inches long so trim off the tip above this length, making a sharp cut just above the level of a leaf. Remove the bottom few leaves that would otherwise go below the level of the soil when the cuttings are planted in the propagating trench. This trench should be in a sheltered part of the garden and is about 7 inches deep with a couple of inches of coarse sand in the bottom. Lean the cuttings against the vertical back of this narrow trench at 2 inch intervals, put the soil back and firm it well down. If you use a hormone rooting powder, make sure it is the correct grade for the hardwood cutting; dip the heel into water before dipping it into the powder. It will be about 12 months before the cuttings are ready to plant out in their flowering positions.

When hardwood cuttings fail it is usually either because they were loose in the soil and not firmed down hard enough or because the trench was in a location which got too much sunshine and dried out too quickly.

Semi-hardwood cuttings

Also called "half-ripe", this group of stem cuttings are taken between July and the middle of September and use new wood which is still soft and supple. Do not choose the softest of the wood—if you can break the stem and still leave some of the soft bark holding it together, then this will be about right. The plants to propagate in this way include buddleia, ceanothus, cotoneaster, escallonia, fuchsia, heathers, hydrangea, potentilla and weigelia.

Again you take off the shoot with a heel from last year's growth and cut off the tip, leaving a shoot about 8 inch long. Cut away the bottom few leaves with a sharp knife and then plant the cutting in a rooting medium made up as before with a mixture of peat, sand and loam. This can be in a sheltered part of the garden frame or in pots placed in the frame. Either way the cuttings should be inserted to a depth of 2 inches and firmed well in. Top moisture is vital and, if you are not using a glass cover, put a polythene bag over the pot. Spraying the foliage helps the cuttings to take and of course the preliminary dip in hormone rooting powder also helps. You will need a different grade to the powder used for the hardwood cuttings as over-stimulation can harm the cutting.

If you grow your cuttings in pots then these should be over-wintered in the cold frame with the covers on, except on good days when they will benefit from some fresh air. The cuttings in the soil of the cold frame will also get the same treatment until the spring when they will be ready to plant out.

Soft-wood cuttings

These cuttings are taken in June and July, when the wood is green and soft and unless you keep them in an environment with plenty of moisture in the atmosphere you will lose many of them. Unfortunately this warm moist atmosphere encourages disease,

Soft wood cuttings benefit from being dipped into a hormone rooting compound before being firmed into the compost.

so start with a good sterile compost, bought from your seedsman or garden centre. Failing this, use a soilless compost made up from vermiculite and incorporating plant foods and trace elements. As you need to keep as much moisture in as possible, the cuttings are best planted in a pot which has been well watered and allowed to drain. There are two ways of preparing soft-wood cuttings, either by making a small heel as previously described or by trimming off the base just below a leaf joint—both methods work and the one you choose is largely a matter of taste. Cuttings are normally 3 or 4 inches long. Cut away the bottom few leaves. Dip it into water and then the appropriate hormone powder. Insert the cutting 1 inch deep and firm it down, put up a small frame of wire over the pot and pull on the polythene bag, which can be fastened under the pot as it will not be removed until the cutting has taken. You will see this by watching the new leaves start to form. Geraniums, deutzia, forsythia, veronicas and many other common plants can be propagated in this way with a minimum of equipment and expense.

Root and leaf cuttings

Root cutting is done by taking a piece of root about 2 inches long and planting it upright with the part taken closest to the stem of the original plant at the top. Cover them with half an inch of compost.

Plants such as Begonia rex are propagated by leaf cuttings. Leaves are taken from the lower part of the plant and laid on a bed of prepared compost. The principal veins on the back of the leaf are cut through, the leaf is laid down with the cuts in contact with the compost and held down with either small stones or wire pins. New plants will form where the cuts have been made provided that you can give the right amount of bottom heat and an overall temperature of 65°F. This is not an easy method, but you may like the challenge.

All of these methods are both simple and successful if the basic rules are followed. Should you not be as "green fingered" as you might have hoped, then look at the things that might have gone wrong. You may have planted too deeply—with soft cuttings only an inch or so needs to go into the compost. Too much water at the start—if you are growing in an enclosed environment (a polythene bag or a propagating frame) then the water in the compost will not be lost for a week or two as long as the cover is on, so don't overwater. Don't let moss grow on the surface of the compost as this will stifle the plant. Finally, remove the cutting from the container once it is established and replant it in a compost that has a higher food content—once you allow the cutting to use up all the available food it will inevitably suffer.

New plants from layers

Layering as done by gardeners is an artificial process but for all that it is very similar to the way in which nature allows shrubs to increase.

The idea is to make the branches of certain shrubs produce new plants while they are still attached to the parent plant.

May and June are the best months although some plants, like

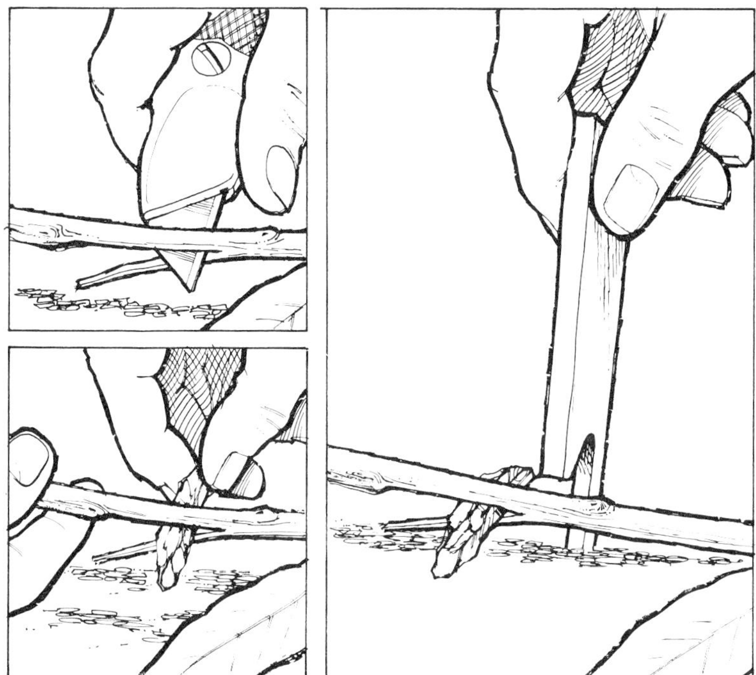

The "layer" is pegged down into John Innes compost to make its own roots before being separated from the parent plant.

wisteria, are layered in the autumn. Once the new plants are well enough established they are separated from the parent and start life on their own. This could well be the following autumn for most layers, but magnolias may take 18 months. Choose a supple, low branch or shoot of young wood and make a slit about an inch long beneath a bud some 12 inch from the tip of the shoot. The slit is held open by means of a small stone and the leaves are removed for three inches or so both sides of the slit. Lay the shoot on the ground and cover the cut portion with a small heap of good soil some 6 inch deep. You may have to hold the shoot down and this is either done with another stone resting on the top of the slit area or with a bent stake of wood or metal.

If your soil is poor then it will pay you to remove some of it and replace it with a mixture of sand, peat and soil then peg the layer down into the new soil. Keep this soil moist until the shoot has rooted and remember to leave the layer attached until a good root structure has formed. Even then it is often advisable to leave the layer for a while after cutting the lead. In many cases this will be the autumn of the same year but with rhododendrons and azaleas you will need to wait an extra year.

Plants that can be propagated in this way include viburnums, magnolias, kalmias, daphnes, cotoneaster, clematis and, of course, the rhododendrons and azaleas.

New plants by division

Plants in your herbaceous border can be increased by division. Perennials should be split every three or four years, the centre part of the plant discarded and the healthy outside parts re-planted.

Dividing perennials is done in either autumn or early spring and of the two the early spring is the better as it is easier to ensure that the portions to be planted have some new shoots on them.

Dividing bulbs

Perhaps the simplest form of propagation. You will have noticed that when you bought good quality bulbs there were often several bulbs joined together at the bottom. These double-nosed bulbs can be split and, if planted in good soil, they will grow in size and each part will put out flower and foliage to rival its parent. Good soil and moisture are vital and if you start with a dozen or two really good bulbs they will soon increase to a grand display. It is this fresh soil that encourages sound growth and explains why bulbs that have been naturalised seldom do as well once the soil around them has become exhausted.

Lilies present a slightly different technique: when planting in the autumn remove two or three plump healthy scales. These are modified leaves which make up the bulb as we know it. With a gentle downward pull break them cleanly away and place them upright in a pot of sandy compost. Just cover with sand, water and place in a cold frame or cool greenhouse. Tiny bulbs will form on the base of the scale and in two or three years' time you should be able to plant out your own home grown lilies.

23

Pruning

GORDON COOPER

There is nothing mysterious about pruning—it is a *practical* procedure developed over the centuries with a practical purpose—there is no magic to it. We prune for three reasons—firstly, by cutting away the old wood we stimulate the growth of new wood; secondly we shape bushes and trees, make them look more attractive; thirdly, we inhibit the spread of disease by cutting away that old and dead wood which is obviously the most vulnerable. Keep these three points in mind and what you do should not be too obscure.

Tools for pruning

The basic tool is the secateur and most gardeners have a pair of one sort or another, but other tools can be useful. Shears for hedges and taking the dead heads from many garden flowers are invaluable in every garden, extension secateurs for pruning branches too high to be reached by either standing on the ground or using a ladder, a pruning saw for cutting thick branches, power saws for the really heavy timber and so on.

But first the secateur. As I have already mentioned it is good policy to buy the best tools you can afford. With good secateurs, pruning becomes that much more easy and there is less danger of splitting the wood and allowing disease and rot to enter the stem. Moreover, a good tool will remain sharp much longer.

Secateurs come in all sorts of shapes and sizes; some work with one cutting blade; this cuts against a fixed anvil and, although it works well, there is a danger of the wood becoming bruised and also little adjustment is possible once the blade becomes worn through use; other types work by having a sharpened blade that cuts past a blunt edge and this produces a good clean cut with a minimum of damage.

When choosing a secateur pick up a pair and see how they feel in your hand, both open and shut. If the garden centre will allow you to cut a piece of branch then you can subject the tool to the best test of all. The cut should be clean and smooth, with both bark and heart cut through without any jagged edges.

Try to clean secateurs after use, and add a drop of oil to the blades and the centre bearing from time to time. Sharpen the blade, if necessary, with a fine grade whetstone and then take up any slack on the centre bearing if your secateur is provided with this refinement.

Where and how to prune

The cut should be made just above a healthy outward facing bud as this keeps the centre of the tree open. Keep the secateurs steady on the branch and do not twist when cutting. The cut should be precisely angled so that it starts opposite the bud and angles towards the top of the bud leaving about $\frac{1}{4}$ inch of stem above it. This angle allows water droplets to run off the stem and so prevents rotting.

If you are pruning large branches from a tree then you will need two cuts with a pruning saw. The first cut is to remove the branch itself and this is done a couple of feet above the position of the final neat cut. By removing the weight of the branch the rest of the job is much easier. The next cut is from below to prevent any bark stripping should the branch fall. The final cut is from above, leaving a small shoulder.

When cutting branches from trees, the wound should be painted over. You can make an effective dressing by mixing white lead and raw linseed oil with a little bordeaux powder, or buy a proprietary compound such as Arbrex. A dark coloured compound is less obtrusive.

Roses

As with every other pruning operation cut away all the dead diseased, weak and mis-shaped wood to start with. This applies to every type of rose, even though they need different treatment

Tall branches can be pruned with a "long arm'.

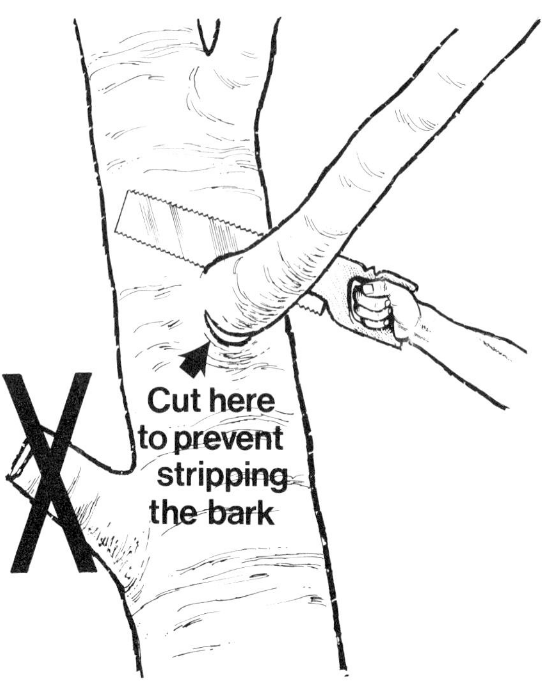

After cutting off large branches always paint the exposed wood with a protective compound to prevent the entry of rot and disease.

afterwards.

Hybrid Tea and Floribunda varieties should be pruned the first spring after planting with the branches cut back to 3 or 4 eyes from the base. Choose an outward facing bud and make your cut just above it. This pruning is best done in February and any roses that you plant after this should be pruned before planting. While on this question of planting it is worth remembering to give the roots a light prune before putting them into the soil. Roots 8–10 inches long are ideal. Do not prune climbing varieties at this time but simply take off a couple of inches or so from the tips.

Once roses are settled in, pruning in later years is more selective. Hybrid Teas should have their strong stems cut to half their length in February and all the poor wood removed as before. I like to give the roses a top prune in the autumn to reduce the

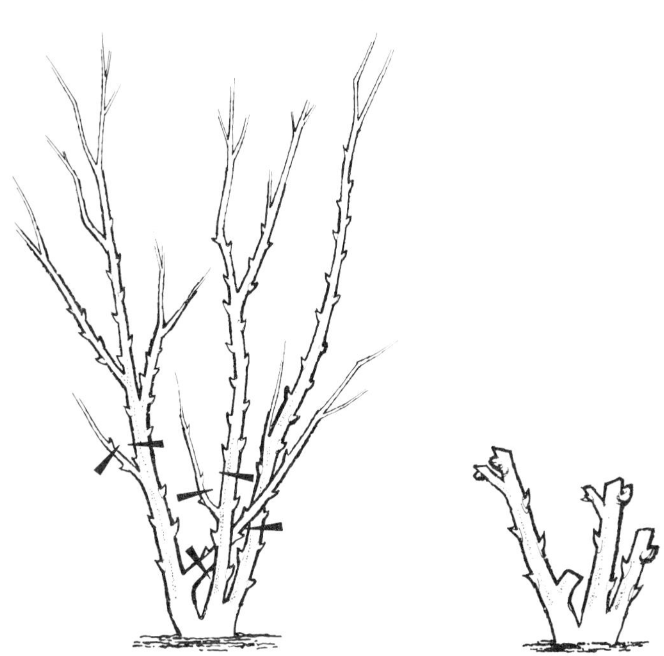

Careful pruning ensures healthy growth and a profusion of bloom.

possibility of their being rocked in the ground by high winter winds.

Floribundas, after the pruning in their first spring, need more careful treatment. The wood put up from the base during the first year needs only light pruning to an outward facing eye, while the wood that has been put up from the stems that were pruned in the first spring can be shortened to half the length of the new wood. In following years it is a continuation of the same technique—cutting the new wood lightly and the older, second year wood, more severely. By pruning this way, you get the longer flowering period which make the Floribundas so popular. This pruning is again done in February and March.

Climbing roses are usually pruned in March but I like to get at them in the autumn to fasten in the new season's growth and cut away a proportion of the old wood. The greater the new growth, the more severe can be the pruning of old wood, but if

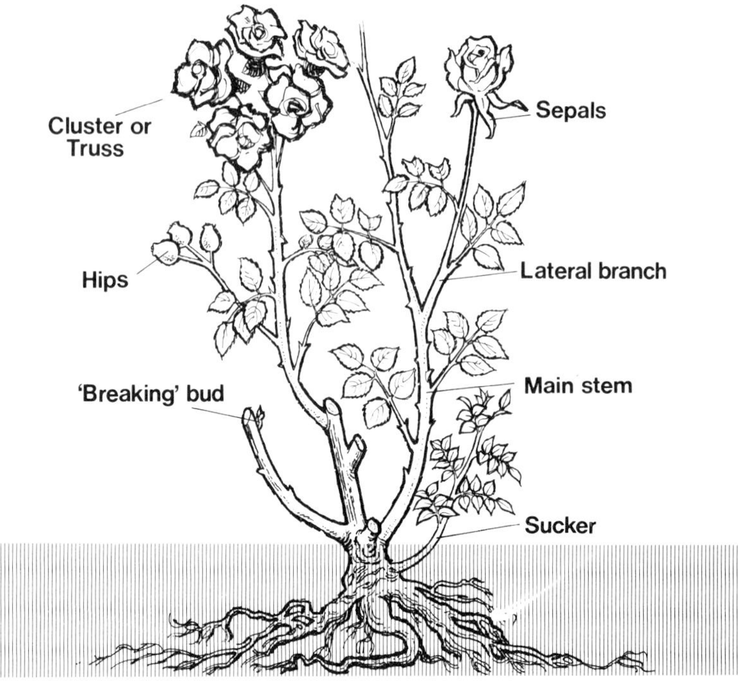

The sucker is growth from the wild rose root stock below the point where the new rose has been grafted. This should be exposed by taking soil away and then tearing the sucker off—not cutting it.

new growth is sparse then be sparing with the secateurs. Also trim back flowered side shoots. This may be unconventional but I do it every year and they don't seem to mind! Ramblers are pruned in the autumn after the rose has flowered and the old wood cut right down to ground level, leaving the new growths which will need tying into supports. It is the new growths that will carry next year's flowers. For shrub roses, again contrary to many textbooks, thin out the older branches. This stimulates new growths.

Miniature roses do not need pruning but they can be trimmed to keep their shape if this becomes necessary after flowering.

Standard roses, and half-standards of course, need severe pruning when first planted, taking the branches back to 3 or 4 eyes in the spring, but in subsequent years only moderate pruning is needed. Aim for a well balanced head with the branches all much the same length and remember that severe pruning will encourage extra growth to the extent that the head may become ungainly.

Two final thoughts on rose pruning. Always burn the wood you have cut away; it will not rot down on the compost heap in any case, but if there is any disease present then burning will prevent its spreading. Secondly, don't be obsessive about when you do it—roses are almost indestructible and a few weeks either way won't ruin them.

Rose suckers are a problem that perhaps comes under this heading, but the last thing you should do is to prune them. These suckers are growths of wild rose from the roots below the graft and the soil should be scraped away to expose the point where the sucker started and it should then be torn away not cut as this may encourage further growth.

Shrubs

To prune shrubs successfully you need to know something about the habit of the plant in question. Casual snipping does more harm than good but if you omit shrub pruning altogether your plants will deteriorate.

Evergreens need little pruning and if you shorten any long or unsightly growths then this is all that is needed.

With deciduous shrubs, that lose their leaves in the winter, you must differentiate between the spring and early summer flowering varieties and those that flower in later summer and early autumn. In the case of the spring and early summer varieties, the blossom comes on wood grown during the previous year, so by pruning as soon as they have finished flowering you are giving the plant a chance to grow new wood during the summer for next year's flower. In this respect, however, I must add that if, like me, you are too harassed in the spring to follow this ideal advice, don't worry—have a go in the autumn, when the leaves have fallen. It's easier to see what you are doing then, in any case. Cut out the flowered wood.

In the case of the late summer and autumn flowering plants, the flower comes on wood produced during the summer so ideally they need to be pruned almost down to the ground during March and April. This will encourage them to put out lots of new shoots that will carry the flower.

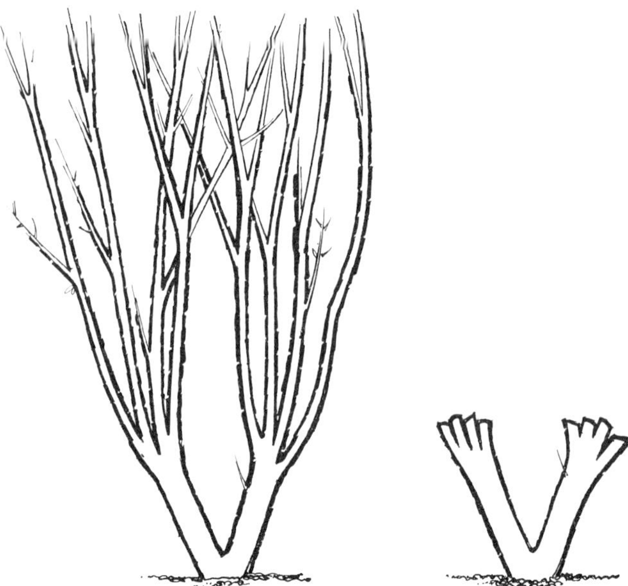

Like other plants that flower on the current season's wood, the Buddleia is cut back so that the last year's growth is reduced to only an inch or so. This is done in the spring so that there is plenty of time for the new, flower-bearing wood to grow.

Once you know when the shrub in question flowers, you are more than half way there and the basic technique involved is much the same as the method we have already examined. Find the right shoot and then cut away the surplus wood.

Those with flowers that come in the first half of the year have the stems cut back to shoots further down the stem. There are one or two exceptions but for deutzia, jasminum nudiflorum, kerria japonica, philadelphus and weigelia this is the method to use. For broom, however, cut back all the stems with seed pods to young shoots. For forsythia aim to cut out about half each year and you will have plenty of blossom. Remember that this plant flowers on wood that is two years old so don't cut it all away.

On the shrubs that flower on new wood later in the summer, you will need some courage if this is the first time you have pruned them. Buddleia davidii, caryopteris, hardy fuchsias, hydrangea paniculata and tamarix can be cut back hard in the spring and they will be all the better for it.

Dead-heading is a summer-long job in the garden but, by taking them off, the plant can concentrate on growing new wood and foliage rather than spending its energy on growing seed heads. For most flowers the dead heads can be cut off but for azaleas and rhododendrons it is better to twist them off, making sure not to harm the new shoots coming from beneath the dead heads. Plants like heathers and helianthemums also need dead heading but the blooms are individually small, so go over them with a pair of shears after they have flowered.

Climbing plants also need pruning and Wisteria needs it twice a year to produce the best of its magnificent blooms. In August cut the young shoots back to six buds from the main stem and then in the winter take them back again to an inch or so in length.

Clematis can be a problem as many gardeners are uncertain about the varieties which they are growing. For pruning purposes they fall into two categories. Jackmanii and viticella varieties have the wood that grew last summer cut back in February to a few buds away from their base and the lanuginosa varieties can be treated in the same way, although in this particular case some authorities suggest that no pruning is needed. With Patens and Montana varieties, however, little pruning is needed; all you need do is cut off the dead heads after flowering as this will encourage a second crop of flower in September. Now can I help you to find out what variety you have. Well, not really, I'm afraid. Catalogue descriptions are too similar to allow for accurate identification. I suggest that all you can do is look carefully at when and how your plant flowers. If it flowers in May or June, as opposed to July or August, the chances are it is a Patens or Montana type. This is not 100 per cent certain but I don't think you'll find any better general guidance. But please don't blame me if I have just ruined the pride of your garden!

Pruning fruit trees

It is always difficult to write about fruit-tree pruning as right from the start one gets involved in the technical terms used to describe the various parts of buds, stems and shoots. In fact, without some knowledge of these terms you will soon finish up with an overgrown orchard—a common cause of dismay to the gardener when he first glances out of the window of the house into which he has just moved.

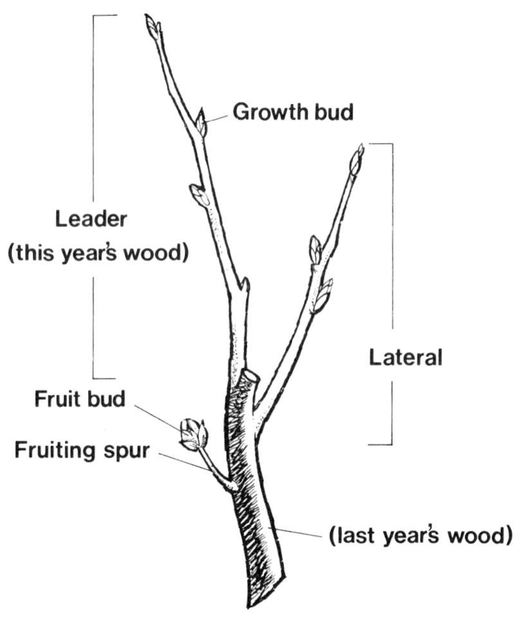

Important parts of the branch to identify when pruning fruit trees.

Let's have a look at some of the more important terms.

Leader: This is this year's growth and it is a straight continuation of the branch.

Lateral: This is the current year's side shoot and it is the lateral that usually carries the fruit. Laterals are described as one year, two year and three year according to their age.

Spur: This is the cluster of fruit which forms on older wood and, if they are overcrowded, small fruit will be the result. Winter pruning should take care of this.

There are two main types of pruning, winter and summer. Winter pruning is concerned with shaping the tree and creating a framework on which fruit can grow. Pruning in winter is to create wood, not fruit; the fact is that while making a well-shaped tree you may discourage fruit for up to five years. When shaping a tree, severe pruning is involved. This means cutting the leaders back by as much as three quarters of their length. Always cut to a bud facing the way in which you want the new leader to grow. This pruning of the leader will encourage the laterals to grow vigorously and they must also be pruned back to within six buds of their base.

Summer pruning is used for apples and pears and the laterals are cut back in late August to six buds of their base to encourage better fruit, as it allows air to circulate within the head of the tree. The pruned laterals are cut back again in the winter.

With new trees planted in the late autumn it is quite safe to cut back the laterals the following spring but if you plant during the spring then leave the job for a year and then cut them hard back.

A note of caution and encouragement

Now we must pause here. Having said so much, I must add that fruit tree pruning is extremely complex; varieties are grouped under certain growing and flowering characteristics and each group requires different pruning. If you want to get the best results, attend carefully to an appropriate handbook. If you don't want the best but still want some fruit on a reasonably shaped tree, I can only give you this advice: you now know why you prune and where you prune—to make the most of this scanty knowledge, pay attention to how and where your particular tree grows, flowers and fruits. Don't prune in such a way that you cut away all the flowering shoots.

If you do this carefully, you will prune quite well, for it is worth repeating that pruning is not a mysterious, obscure practise—people have learned to prune properly in the past by doing just what I am suggesting you can do—that is, observing carefully *how* and *when* and *where* a plant or tree grows and flowers.

Particular pruning techniques

Apple Trees. Once your apple trees are established and well shaped, ready to bear fruit, then pruning is a matter of shortening the laterals in November to two or three buds from the main stem and shortening the leaders by about one third of their length. When the tree is fruiting well it is advisable to reduce the number of fruit to two per spur and in this way you will get better, larger fruit. This thinning should be done at the end of June after the infertile fruitlets have been shed. (This we refer to as the "June drop".)

Pears. Treatment is much the same as for apples, with the laterals being shortened to five leaves over a period of several weeks during July and August. Winter pruning is also much the same but fruit thinning must be less drastic, as many pears will fall of their own accord during the spring and summer.

Blackberries, Loganberries and Raspberries. Immediately after the fruit has been picked the old wood is cut away to ground level and the new wood tied in position.

Blackcurrants. Prune right after fruiting and cut away the old wood that carried the fruit. The fruit comes on new wood and, by taking the old growth out right back to the point it grew from, you will encourage new shoots and a good crop next year.

Red and White Currants. On established bushes prune in the winter when the plant is dormant, taking off the shoots so that only six inches is left of the new wood. Side shoots are cut back to one bud as this encourages the spurs which provide the fruit. As with apples, cutting back the leader will encourage side shoots, so this should also be done.

Gooseberries. Prune in the autumn by tipping the leaders and taking out any wood growing into the centre of the bush. Most of the side shoots can be left but some of them can be shortened back to one bud from the base.

Peaches. Peaches flower on the wood produced during the previous year and also on short spurs, so with trees that are growing in the open rather than against a wall it is advisable to prune in April when the trees are in leaf. Cut away old, hard wood as this will encourage new shoots. Your aim is to have an open centred tree, with three or four main branches growing up through the heart of it, and once you have achieved this framework over the first three years of the tree's growth it will start to bear fruit. Heavy pruning is desirable as otherwise a tree will be inclined to overbear and the quality of the fruit will suffer. This means hard thinning so careful selection of the shoots that are to be left is desirable.

First remove all the spindly shoots and then cut back the hranched shoots to an outward facing bud or sturdy lateral. By doing this you will encourage new shoots and also allow the tree to carry the amount of fruit that it can cope with.

Plums. Plums should be pruned during the summer after the crop has been taken off. Any large cuts should be painted over right away to prevent silver leaf disease getting at the tree but, in the main, routine pruning will be light rather than severe once the tree has been trained to a good shape over the first five years of growth. During this period the leaders can be cut back to half their length to produce a well shaped head, strong enough to carry heavy crops.

After this a light prune in the summer, in which the vertical shoots are tipped and some of the side shoots removed, will be enough.

24

The lawn

GORDON COOPER

There are many books and pamphlets on lawns, so why do I include them in this book, which I hope is largely devoted to the more intriguing aspects of gardening? There are two reasons. Firstly the averagely lazy gardener is more likely to be distressed by his lawn than anything else and, secondly, preparing and laying a lawn is a once for all job, which is worth doing right, since there is no second chance. The trouble is that a lawn is so fundamental to a garden that most people hurry in laying it—they understandably feel that they don't have a garden until they get the grass down. So they skimp, and undoubtedly live to regret it. Many is the time I have been asked to advise on poor lawns only to find on enquiring that the owners had not *exactly* laid the seed onto builder's rubble but . . . well they had done the next best (or rather, worst) thing.

It is so often said that such and such bit of hard work is "worth it in the long run", and I often feel that such advice probably rings rather falsely to the average gardener. So take me seriously this time, when I advise you in this manner when it comes to lawns.

The sad fact is that even to maintain a good lawn involves much hard work. Square yard for square yard grass requires more work and treatment than almost any other sort of cultivation. For remember that grass is a perennial plant, one that grows year after year; in some parts of the country, indeed, it is hardly dormant during the winter at all. With this amount of constant growth, it is easy to see that both the soil conditions supplied at the outset and the yearly maintenance must be good.

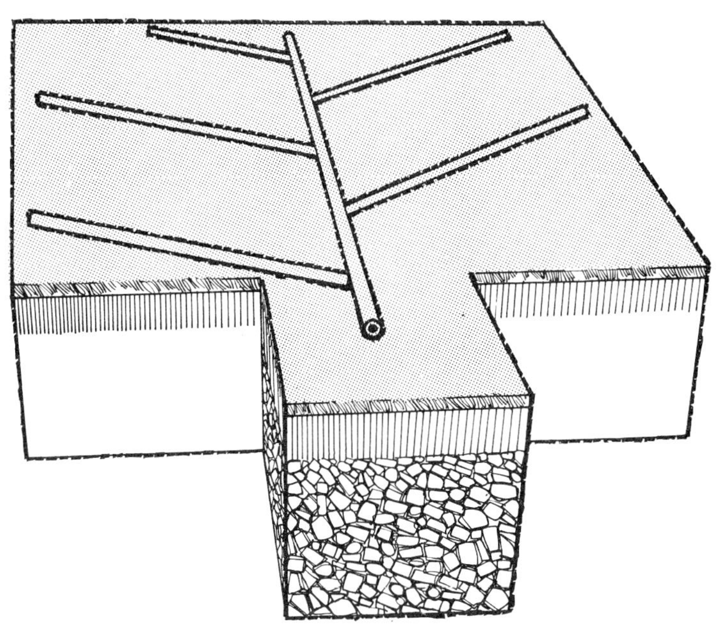

Drainage pipes should take the water towards the soakaway at the lowest part of the garden.

Drainage

Grass does not like waterlogged soil and you must make up your mind before preparing the soil if the drainage you have is adequate. If your soil is really heavy, you may have to install a drainage system, using earthenware pipes sunk 2 feet deep into the soil and covered with clinker. These pipes are laid in a herring-bone pattern with the central pipe going from the top part of the site towards the lowest point, where a soakaway is constructed. The side pipes lie parallel to each other, running downhill to join onto the main central pipe at 10 feet intervals.

An alternative method is to take off the top soil and cover the site with broken clinker, coarse ashes and broken bricks to a depth of four inches. Over this put some more ashes and any bulky material available, to prevent the top soil running away when put back. At the lowest part of the garden build a soakaway and cover this with a few inches of soil as well.

Soil preparation

Turn over the topsoil to a depth of nine inches or so as deep as your subsoil will allow. Treat the soil as you go along with peat, compost or well rotted manure if your soil is light or sandy, and sand or coke ash if the soil is heavy. Really heavy clay will take up to 14 lb. of sand to the square yard.

Lawns can be made from turf or sown with seed. Turf is faster and the preparation of the soil is not so critical. In fact, provided that you let the ground settle and trample it down to remove bumps and hollows as described on the following page, the preliminary digging described above is sufficient. Finally, turf can be laid at almost any time of the year, although it is generally done during the winter. The disadvantages to set against the above are that turf is more expensive and the lawn will not be of such high quality, unless you buy seed-sown turf, which is expensive. Weed-free turf is almost impossible to get and it will take some time to eliminate the weeds.

Seed, on the other hand is less expensive per square yard and a seedsman can provide you with blends of seed to meet different requirements. Now for the type of seed to choose. Most advice on this subject, it seems to me, misses a fundamental point and is therefore quite misleading. The distinction is always drawn between cheaper mixtures, containing "rye" grass, and the more expensive mixtures, of "bent" and "fescue" grasses, and is drawn in terms of appearance and toughness. The more expensive mixtures are said to give finer-looking lawns but not to wear so well; the cheaper rye mixtures are tough but look coarse.

Half of this distinction, however, is not really valid—if the mixture is primarily of bent grasses, then its durability is not at all bad. After all, Wimbledon tennis courts are turfed with such mixtures. Combine this misconception with another fact, generally overlooked, and we get a startling endorsement of more expensive bent mixtures. This fact is that rye grass grows about twice as fast as finer-leaf grasses and all that rather formidable mowing described later on becomes even more demanding. My firm advice, therefore, all other things being equal, is to choose a mixture of bent grasses—the extra expense is negligible and it will serve for most domestic use.

But of course there are drawbacks to all seed. Sowing times are more restricted and April or late summer are to be preferred. Once germination has started there must be no drying out and the generally plentiful rainfall of spring and late summer help us here. Lawns sown with seed need a few months to consolidate and settle down before they can be used. (Note, however, the several fast growing varieties, such as Summerday, that produce a fine effect in only a few weeks. The speed of growth then declines so that a lot of cutting is not needed, but there is still a delay before the surface is firm enough for general use.) Birds can cause considerable damage and look for a seed treated with bird repellant. Damping off (see p. 169) is another trouble and the weather itself can make it difficult to maintain ideal growing conditions.

Once the preliminary digging has been done you must allow three or four weeks for the soil to settle. This cannot be left to happen on its own, for the lumps that were left will soon show as humps on the lawn surface. The soil, therefore, must be broken up: trampling over it on your heels works well, as your own weight helps the soil to consolidate and you will feel any stones which should be taken off. As previously mentioned, this also applies to ground which is to be turfed, but it is clearly more important when seeding is envisaged. Alternatively, you can go over the site with a roller, then rake it and then go over it with a roller again, but you can only do this when the soil is dry. Once the site has been dug over and firmed down the next step is to break it down into a fine tilth suitable for a seed bed, with even more raking and treading down. A firm, even crumb structure is thus achieved.

At this stage you have a site ready for sowing but if you are aiming for the best possible lawn of fine grasses spend a few months more during the summer in "fallowing" the site. I say this, but am well aware that most of you will probably not go to this extent, reckoning that it is better to get on with it and then remove the weeds with weedkillers at a later stage. "Fallowing" involves going over the site at monthly intervals to remove all the weeds that have been dormant during the preliminary preparation. A programme of raking to encourage their growth, and hoeing to kill them will achieve the desired result and the site will be ready for sowing during the latter part of August or early September—almost 12 months from the time when you started. If you don't fallow, you can either turf or sow during April or May.

How to sow

Application rates are critical and it is worth marking out your site with string to break it up into square yards. Seed is sown at the rate of 1½–2 oz. per square yard and if you choose a day when the soil is fairly dry and there is no wind you will have no trouble in ensuring an even application. You can, of course, apply seed with a spreader but be careful to cover all the surface and not leave gaps between each traverse of the spreader or go over the same strip twice.

After sowing, rake the soil over the seed lightly and then ensure that it does not dry out during the first ten days when germination is taking place. After this period. you may find both grass and weeds growing up together and within the next fourteen days it is possible to treat the weeds with a special "Weedkiller for New Lawns" that will kill the weeds without affecting the new grass. Do not use the same selective weedkiller that you use on an established lawn as this is far too strong for the grass seedlings.

The first cutting can be done with a mower with well sharpened and properly adjusted blades set high, once the grass is about 2 inch tall. Take care to ensure that your mower is set properly or you will damage the grass and blunt blades will pull the grass out of the ground. This first cut will also kill most of the annual weeds.

How to turf

Buy your turf from a reliable source and specify "treated turves" as this will minimise the amount of weed even if it does not eliminate it. Turves are a standard size of 3 × 1 foot and cut to a uniform depth. They will probably be delivered rolled up and if you are not going to lay them in just a few days they should be unrolled as otherwise they will turn yellow. If they are left rolled there is also a danger of stretching the roots, and once the turves loose their standard size it becomes more difficult to lay them in a regular pattern.

When laying turf it is advisable to stand on a long plank: this prevents the soil being compressed further and stops the soil collecting on your feet. This plank can be moved off the soil onto the first row of laid turves and it then helps to press the turves onto the soil. Work across the site laying in rows and bonding the turves like bricks with the joins in one row meeting the centre of the turf laid in the next row. Make sure that the turves are as close together as possible; any gaps left can be filled in with sand or sifted soil.

After a few days roll the lawn with a light roller and make sure that the turves do not dry out, as this will cause them to shrink and you will have more gaps to fill. Cutting should be delayed until growth is evident and then only a light trim is required.

How to mow

Once the lawn is established and growing well, the technique of proper mowing must be considered. Ideally the grass should be much the same height throughout the year and this can only be done by *regular* cutting to a height which encourages the grass to grow strongly. Infrequent cutting, which often means that you cut it very short to compensate for your idleness, reduces the strength of the grass and allows moss, daisies and pearlwort to become established; a long gap until the next mowing means that the coarser weeds will also thrive at the expense of the grass.

Unless you are using a rotary mower, which tends to leave little trace of its path, the way you cover the lawn will determine the final appearance—all those lovely stripes of the traditional English lawn.

To get the lines, start with a pattern in mind. First of all go up and down the short edges twice as this will give you space in which to turn the machine round and then work backwards and forwards along the longer dimension of the lawn. The diagram gives a useful scheme. From time to time mow the other way and make the lines run at ninety degrees to the usual cut. This helps you keep the grass growing vertically, rather than the leaning effect you may create if you always cut in the same direction.

When cutting with a rotary machine, work around the outside edge of the lawn and then move gradually towards the centre, with each ever decreasing circle just overlapping the previous one.

With many of the rotary mowers you will leave the cuttings all over the lawn behind you and, except in very dry spells when they can act as a mulch after they have been evenly spread over the lawn, they should be swept up and used in making compost. (See also comments on the Flymo in the next section.) The only time when you cannot do this is immediately after you have

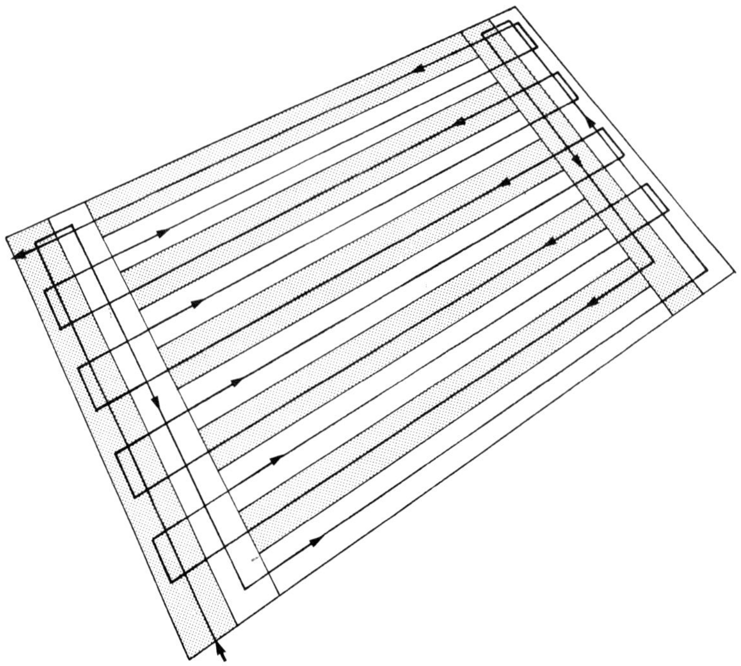

By working to this pattern for one cut and then in the opposite direction for the second cut you will have both lines and an evenly growing lawn.

treated the lawn with a selective weedkiller. Cuttings of this sort must not go onto the compost heap. If you leave normal cuttings on the lawn, in wet weather they turn the grass beneath an unpleasant yellow and encourage worm casts and fungus diseases. Any weed seed that you might have trimmed off will also have a chance to germinate. Finally, lumps of grass don't look nice and eventually clog the lawn seriously.

What sort of mower

Side wheel mowers tend to be the cheapest and often the lightest in use but you cannot cut right to the edge of the lawn with them. As they have no front roller, however, they are fine for weeds, and perhaps for really sappy, fast growing varieties of grass. A better general purpose machine is one with a roller on the back which stretches the full width of the machine. You can cut over the edges of the lawn with a model of this sort and the rolling action gives a good finish to the job. Mowers come in many sizes; for the average garden, 12 inch or 14 inch is enough; with the wider machine there is some difficulty of manoeuvering and this can more than offset the pleasure of getting the job done quickly. Power mowers of the blade type with conventional cutting cylinders are available driven by petrol, petrol and oil mixture, electricity and battery. An important and generally overlooked aspect is the capacity and design of the grass box. Ideally it needs to be both large and to be of such a design that the cuttings do not fall back onto the blades even when it is only half full.

Rotary machines are most effective but they do not provide such a good finish. They will tackle rough grass, that the conventional cylinder machine will not look at. Most models operate on wheels but the Flymo works on a cushion of air and this enables it to tackle banks and cut under low shrubs very effectively. It is worth noting that the cuttings of the Flymo are small and widely scattered. If the grass is cut frequently it is not easy to rake up. The makers claim that you don't need to, which may be true in general, though at some stage you will have to rake them all up. Incidentally, there is also a rotary mower which sucks the lot up, twigs and all—it is expensive but if it tempts you, I am not surprised!

Recovering a bad lawn

Before looking at the ways in which lawns are maintained by correct feeding, watering, spiking and dressing it is worth looking at the lawn we may already have and which is less perfect than it should be. In the really severe case where moss, low growing weeds and patches of bare earth are more numerous than the amount of grass still growing, the only course of action is to start again. Dig the site over and follow the instructions already given for making a new lawn.

In other cases where the problem is not beyond treatment it is important to establish just what is the trouble. Weeds in such abundance that the grass does not have a chance can be brought under control by regular cutting and treatment with selective weedkillers, which tackle the broad-leaved weeds but do not harm the lawn grasses. Weeds can also be taken out by hand or with a daisy grubber. Spot chemicals can be applied to individual

Fertilisers, selective weedkillers and granulated moss killers are best applied with a special lawn spreader which ensures even distribution.

weeds or areas of trouble without going over the whole lawn area.

Moss often appears on badly maintained lawns. Too little lime, poor drainage, insufficient fertiliser, too much shade and too severe cutting, all are likely to promote moss. You must determine the cause of the trouble if you are to avoid a recurrence. Meanwhile, treat the moss with a moss killer based on mercury, or with lawn sand in the spring. Once the moss is dead, rake it off the lawn.

Most other weeds will respond to either hormone weed killers or lawn sand but if your overgrown lawn has clumps of broad leaved grasses in it then these must be dug out and new soil and seed put in.

A healthy lawn must be fed from time to time and in this

recovery operation it is safe to assume that this has not been done for some time. A compound fertiliser such as Lawn Plus will put into the soil a balanced range of foods to encourage good growth and then you must keep up the regular cutting. Once this has set a pattern of growth for the lawn you can start to eradicate the weeds with selective weed killer. Several of these incorporate plant foods so that the grass grows while the weeds die. Evergreen 80 is a good example of this type of chemical. Once started, this feeding must be continued.

Aerating lawns

You must also make sure that the soil is in good condition to support the grass and you must start the process of regular spiking and raking the lawn. This is to aerate it to allow both air and moisture to get to the roots. Aerating can be done by driving a fork into the soil to a depth of four inches and covering the whole area of the lawn so that there are holes at six inch intervals all over it. A better method is to use a hollow-tined fork that pulls out plugs of soil that are swept up when the spiking is finished. Another method is to fix a spiked roller to the back of the mower and draw this all over the lawn surface. Aeration keeps the grass healthy and allows air, water and fertilisers to get below the surface. It must surely be one of the most neglected but essential jobs in lawn care. It is a long-term operation—don't expect the grass to spring up immediately!

Aerating is done in the autumn and if you have any bare patches on the lawn this is the time to roughen up the soil surface (scarifying) and sow new seed. At least once each year, and more if you use a rotary mower, you should also rake all dead matter from the lawn. This also helps fertilisers and water to reach the roots; dead grass etc., is quite absorbent.

Watering the lawn

In a normal year there is enough rainfall about to keep the grass growing happily. In drought situations steps must be taken right away to ensure that the lawn, which loses *more than a gallon of water per square yard every day*, has an ample supply to maintain steady growth. The first sign of water shortage is that the tops of the grass start to go brown. This means that the soil is dry to a depth of four inches where the roots are and unless you start

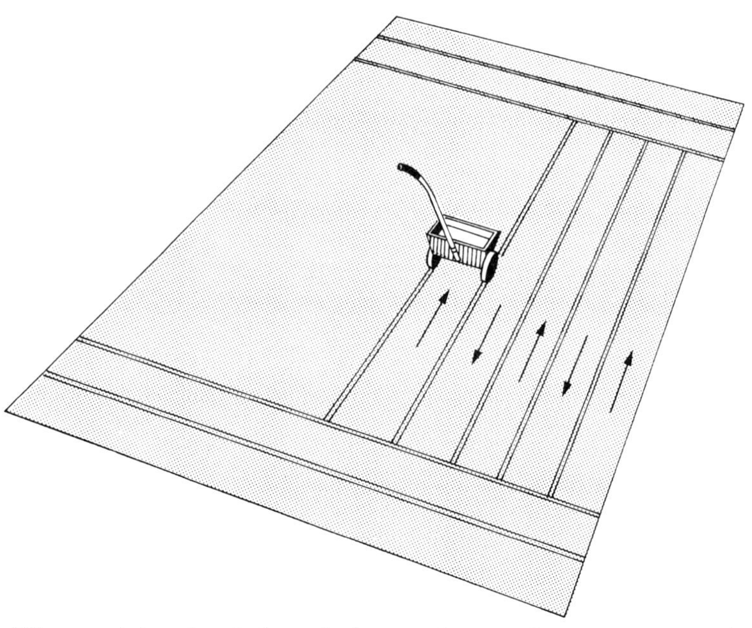

When applying chemicals to the lawn make sure that your traverses do not overlap.

artificial watering *right away* the roots may well die. Another trouble invariably comes at the same time in the form of clover which thrives under these dry or very dry conditions. When you water, remember that the moisture must penetrate the top four inches of soil, so it needs a really good soaking. A light wetting on the top does more harm than good even though the grass may look better for a day or two. The water must get down to the roots.

Feeding the lawn regularly

Grass, like any other growing plant, uses certain chemicals in its growth and, unless these are replaced as they are taken out, the lawn will suffer and the grass will die. As grass does not grow at the same rate throughout the year it needs different foods at different times, so a three stage feeding programme is the ideal—the application of a balanced fertiliser in the spring, in June and again in September. There are several balanced or "compound" fertilisers on the market and the packet will contain application details. It is worth investing in a special applicator, rather than relying on broadcast methods. This enables you to apply the fertilisers regularly. Take care not to overlap, as shown in the diagram.

Top dressings

And here is a final task for the perfectionist.

A lawn is a highly concentrated perennial plant growth. The roots go down only four inches so everything that happens on the surface has a bearing on the health and vitality of the plant. Make up a mixture of 4 parts loam, 2 parts sand and 1 part peat and brush this into the grass after spreading it at the rate of 2 lb. per square yard. Compost from the garden heap also makes a fine top dressing. The grass will soon grow through it and it can also be used for levelling up any minor hollows in the lawn surface. This dressing is best applied in the spring and makes the top few inches of soil open and healthy. If your soil is sandy then the amount of peat can be doubled to hold water near the surface.

Well, that's that. Is all that work worth it to you? The fact is, of course, that the vast majority say "no" and decline such hard labour. Unfortunately the other fact is that a really fine lawn does need such care—it is a cruel world, indeed!

25

A note on weeds, pests and disease

GORDON COOPER

Weeds on paths and areas where no plants at all are to grow can be dealt with by using one of several weedkillers applied by watering can. Flame guns will do the job also, for they tend to burn both the plant and its seed, but if you have only a small area then the cost of the gun may well discourage you, even though it is great fun!

Useful chemical weedkillers are Weedex and Sodium Chlorate. Weedex is based on simazine and operates by creating a barrier which kills weed seeds as they germinate. After application to clean soil no disturbance must take place as weeds will commence to grow again. Weedex is fine on paths and is perhaps to be preferred to sodium chlorate which does the same job. This chemical can be dangerous—splashes of the solution on clothes make them extremely inflammable when the material has dried out.

For less permanent weeding there is Weedol, and this must not be confused with Weedex as its action is totally different. Weedol is based on paraquat and is watered on to green foliage in order to kill the weed; it will also kill any plants it touches as it is not selective in any way. Weedol works by using energy from daylight to kill the weeds through their leaves; it becomes inert once it touches the soil so there is no residual problem. By using a special sprinkler bar attached to the watering can, the fluid can be applied very accurately, but avoid windy days as the wind can blow it onto plants you wish to keep.

Selective weedkiller is used on lawns to kill the broad-leaved weeds while not harming the narrow leaved grasses. The hormone types work by encouraging the weeds to outgrow their strength; this characteristic worries some gardeners, since after application the weeds seem to thrive, but after a few days they die. Mixtures containing Fenoprop or Mecoprop are effective in controlling clover. On new lawns a more gentle chemical is "Weedkiller for New Lawns" which is based on morfamquat; although the normal selective weedkiller is perfectly sound it would be too strong for tender new grass. It is also worth bearing in mind that fertilisers like Lawn Plus and Evergreen 80 are a blend of both plant food and selective weedkiller so that, while you are putting down the weeds, you are encouraging the grass to grow and fill up the spaces left by the dead weeds.

One final word on weedkillers, and that concerns dealing with couch grass in beds—a real problem once it gets a hold. Dalapon is most effective.

Types of weeds

But, when all is said and done, it is the hoe which is your main weapon against weeds in flower beds etc. Keep at them—a little and often is the way. Don't wait until they are thriving great brutes. There are two main sorts of weeds that you will hoe up—annual and perennial.

Annual weeds are exasperating but are at least controllable. The deep rooted ones illustrated here are a perennial nightmare, they require ruthless digging, poisoning and hoeing (it is amazing how quickly they become weakened by just hacking their tops off every time a green shoot appears). Now, at least you will be able to recognise your enemies.

Pests and disease

Why worry if your roses have a few greenfly? They will still come out and the greenfly may even go away. Similarly why worry if you dig up some of those rather revolting chafer grubs? True, they feed on the plants but plants are quite tough and there may not be too many of them. And caterpillars? Yes, they eat the leaves etc., but remember also that they turn into butterflies. While we are on insects—how many delightful ladybirds are those greenfly of yours supporting. Spray them with insecticide and what will happen to the ladybirds?

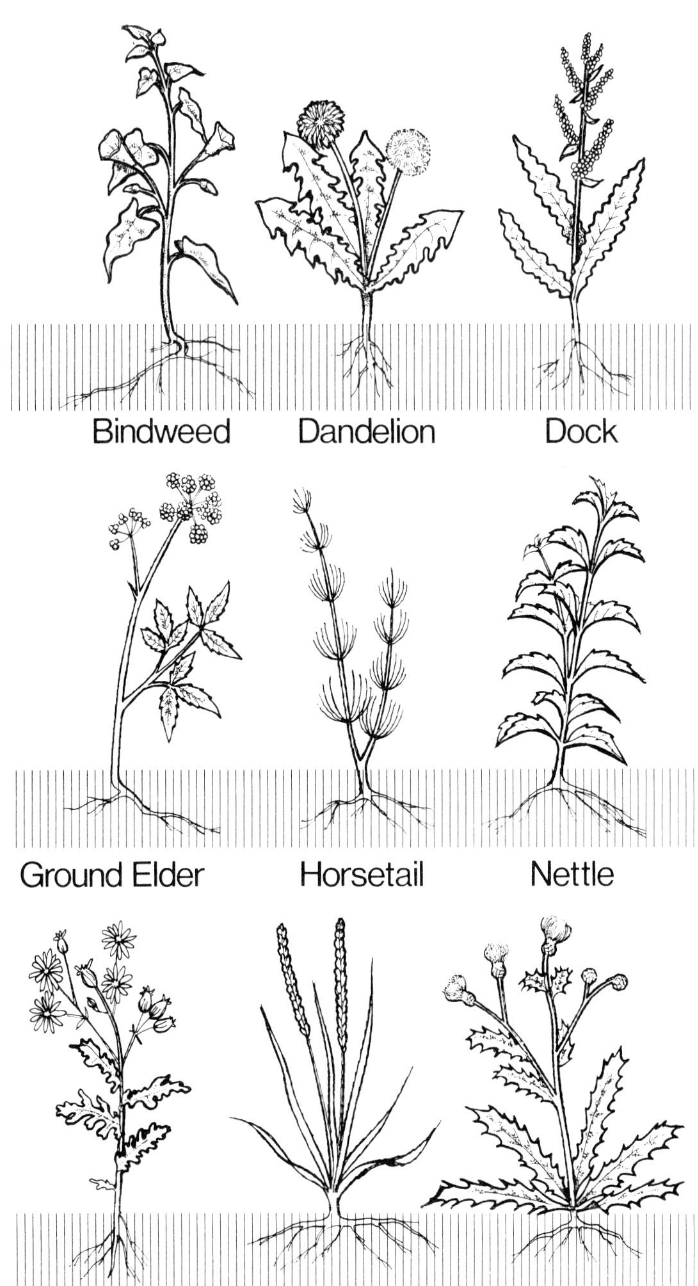
Bindweed
Dandelion
Dock
Ground Elder
Horsetail
Nettle
Ragwort
Twitch/Couch
Thistle

What I am saying is simple. Don't be too obsessive about pests and disease.

If something persistent and serious occurs then of course you will need to take action. But remember, for this to be effective it can be costly, and while you are waging war against the foes of the garden, its friends may also suffer.

There are two tips I can give. First, grow your plants well; a vigorous plant is less prone to disease. Secondly, keep a tidy garden. Has it ever occurred to you how many pests may be lurking under that pile of old rubbish in the corner?

Opposite: All these perennial weeds must be burned and not put on the compost heap.

26

Hedging

GORDON COOPER

New gardens get smaller as the price of building land increases and the increased need for a little privacy is provided by hedges, fences and screens. You may also want to sit in the sun out of the wind. This is another once and for all job—mistakes here are difficult to rectify, so it really pays to do it well.

Fences are covered in chapter 17. More attractive than these are hedges, and there is also a further point that is well worth noting. Air striking the solid face of a fence bounces up and then swirls over and down. A solid hedge, however, absorbs much of the air. Thus, unless we are talking about a howling gale, hedges provide better protection from the wind in many instances.

First you must prepare the soil, bearing in mind that the plants you put in are closely packed and are going to be there for a long time. This means deep digging to a depth of 12 inches, or deeper if your soil allows it, even up to two feet. But do not bring up the subsoil. Work plenty of well rotted manure and compost into the bottom of the area you turn over. The prepared strip of soil must be wide enough to provide a good root run for the plants and it is not enough to simply turn over the soil along the length of the proposed hedge in a form of a narrow trench a foot wide. No, make it at least 24 inches and preferably 36 inches of good rich soil, to encourage deep, wide rooting.

If your hedge is to be evergreen plants then do the planting in October to mid-November or mid-March to April. Deciduous plants that lose their leaves in winter can be planted over a longer period, from say November to March, but the job can only be done satisfactorily when the soil is in a workable condition—you you will never firm the soil down properly if it is in big, wet chunks. You will need a lot of plants for a hedge, although the amount will depend on the variety you choose. In any case a new hedge can be expensive so if you run into a dry spell after planting remember to water to keep the plants growing. Cold spells in the winter can do damage, particularly to evergreens, so have some protection in the form of sacking that can be draped on poles on the windward side of really valuable plants to keep the wind off.

Once you have the hedge growing well, don't ignore it. Like any other growing thing it will need feeding and watering. A slow acting fertiliser once a year and a mulch with either compost or peat will be well worth the trouble. Cutting is another routine job—the small-leaved hedges such as privet need a clipping from time to time with sharp shears; broad-leaved plants should be cut with secateurs rather than shears, which slice through the leaves.

Which hedge to choose

There is, of course, a big selection and you can be adventurous. These are my selection. If you want a fast screen, using conifers, then Cupressocyparis Leylandii is the best of the lot, growing as much as four feet in a year, while Cupressus macrocarpa lutea is also fast and particularly good in coastal areas. Thuya plicata Coles variety and Chamaecyparis, Croftway green (see Plant Names), are also effective screening plants. All these should be planted at 2½ foot intervals. A sort of evergreen is the Beech, with its russet leaves lasting through the winter until pushed off by next season's growth.

A good hedge can be made by blending evergreen and semi-evergreen shrubs and interplanting some flowering shrubs grown as standards so that their heads stay above the body of the hedge. Cotoneaster frigida, ceanothus, eleagnus ebbingii and prunus laurocerasus make a good hedge body to which can be added trees with twiggy heads such as prunus pissardii, prunus blireana, cratageus, malus and salix. Investigate all these. Roses of course, make good hedges. Some of the shrub roses such as Nevada and Fruhlingsgold grow quickly into an impenetrable barrier and the taller floribunda roses also do a good job. I have seen a hedge of Queen Elizabeth over eight feet tall that would stop almost anything.

Privet is still a deservedly popular hedging plant, particularly in areas where industrial activity makes the air dirty. It is a quick grower even on windy sites but instead of the common ligustrum ovalifolium try the golden privet, ligustrum aureum, as its bright colour is a cheering sight in the middle of winter. Privets of all sorts are, of course, phenomenally cheap when compared to most other hedging plants.

27

Garden produce

GORDON COOPER

Growing your own vegetables and fruit certainly saves money that may well be the guiding reason for some people. But not for many, I suggest. In this respect the trouble is that so often when you have a fine crop of lettuce so does everybody else and there is a glut on the market. No, I am sure that for most of us the compelling reason is that we like it: we like the freshness of garden vegetables and fruit, we like the blossom of fruit trees, we like the look of those neat rows of cabbages in the brown earth, we like the very idea of using our land in such a fundamental fashion. It is this delight in growing things which is significant to me—it may be the case that produce is not grown in most gardens but none can deny that, in a very special way, such cultivation is what it's all about. And so it must be included in this book.

The vegetable garden

First, look at the space available. You might think it better to grow some of the more unusual vegetables that you cannot get from the greengrocers such as celeriac, sweet corn, parsley and of course some of the herbs such as mint, chives, or marjoram to help in the kitchen. It is up to you of course, but a vegetable garden is a great opportunity for a little adventure and innovation.

Whatever you grow, preparation of the soil is most important as usual. With heavy cropping you are taking a lot out of the soil. For this reason also a three or four year cycle of crops has become standard practice; rotation of this sort rests the ground and enables one plant to work for another. If you grow the same crop on the same piece of ground every year it will get worse and worse as the soil gets exhausted.

When digging the soil, work in plenty of manure except in the space where you are proposing to grow carrots and parsnips. Lime can be applied every three years or so to keep the soil sweet but if your soil is chalky this may not be necessary.

Vegetable propagation

Vegetables from seed. This is the largest group of vegetables and includes peas and beans, beet, carrot, lettuce, onions, parsley, parsnips, radish, spinach, swede and turnips. Soil preparation is the same as for any other seed sown in the open garden in that the soil must be broken down to a fine crumb structure. Traditionally, sowing for many varieties is done *in situ* in shallow drills and the seedlings are thinned out when they are large enough to handle. This thinning enables the remaining plants to grow properly without having to struggle for air, moisture and food. Do not, therefore sow the seeds too thinly; make allowance that some of the seeds may not germinate. The depth of the seed varies according to its size but roughly three times the length is about right. Then the drill is drawn over the seed and the bed is watered.

It cannot be denied, however, that the above mentioned thinning out is tiresome. Thereafter, whatever crop you intend, my advice is to use a pelletted seed. These cost a little more but each seed is surrounded with a coating of fungicide and fertiliser which greatly enhances its chances of successful germination. Also the seeds are easier to space.

As described above, about half the common vegetables grown from seed germinate and flower in the same bed. Some, however, need more specialised treatment. Cabbages, cauliflower, sprouts, broccoli, lettuce and leeks are grown by starting them off from seed in a seed bed, from which the plants are transferred into the vegetable garden proper when they are sufficiently grown. Sweet corn, marrows, tomatoes and celery are started under glass and not transferred outside until the danger of frost is over.

For the varieties that are sown outside, soil preparation is as before but the drills can be closer, say 6 inches apart as the plants will only be there while they are small. Once you can handle them without trouble, the seedlings go into the vegetable garden into the positions they are to occupy until harvested. Lift them carefully from underneath by inserting a small fork and lifting gently. At this stage the cabbage plants may be 4 inches tall and fairly tough but the lettuces may be only an inch or so tall and have very little root structure. Plant them in rows allowing enough space between each plant for it to be able to grow comfortably. Make a small hole with a dibber, drop the roots in and firm the soil down.

The seeds sown under cover are ideally transferred into peat pots, once they are large enough to handle, and then planted out of doors when the frost danger is over. By using peat pots of this sort the final transplanting of both plant and pot together avoids any setback to the roots and the plant grows away strongly.

One final point for those who have small gardens. Peas, broad beans, cabbage and lettuce, particularly the first two, can grow to unwieldy proportions. Remember that you can get smaller varieties of these vegetables, much more suited to small plots.

Vegetables from tubers and bulbs. Onions, shallots, potatoes, Jerusalem artichokes and garlic are examples of this sort of vegetable but the treatment of each varies; potato and artichoke need to be covered with 4 inches of soil but onions, shallots and garlic are pressed into the surface soil. The onions I refer to are those grown from "sets", which are really baby onions.

Planned growing

Growing for succession. By careful planning it is possible to stretch the use of your vegetables over a long period. Not simply leaving them in the ground where they go tough and coarse but by sowing at three week intervals. Instead of putting all the seed in at the same time and having too big a crop all at once, sow only a third of your seed and then repeat the treatment twice more. An alternative method is to sow early, mid season and late varieties of the same crop. With peas this might mean sowing Feltham First as an early, Early Onward as a mid-season and Rentpayer as a late variety.

In a small plot it is worth intercropping. This means that you grow two crops on the same patch of ground, by mixing up varieties which grow quickly with those that mature more slowly. You might sow radishes and lettuce between the rows of peas and beans as they will have been harvested before the peas and beans need the space. Another space you can use is the tops of the ridges left when planting celery. You can plant radishes, lettuce and even French Beans here without affecting the main crop.

Catch crops are another essential in concentrated vegetable growing. These are fast growing crops that are put into the ground between harvesting one crop and starting the next. As the leeks do not go into the ground until June, you could sow broad beans in November, harvest them in June and then put the leeks in. Lettuce, radish and spinach are also useful catch crops, filling up even shorter gaps because of their faster growing time.

Vegetable seeds are controlled by the 1920 Seeds Act which lays down minimum germination and purity percentages. This guarantees that out of every 100 seeds of Brussels sprouts 70 will germinate, and that with cauliflower you will get 60 out of every 100 to germinate; for other seeds the percentages vary. This is only a part of the story and many of the best strains of seed are the result of careful selection, so buy them from good reliable companies—at least they have their reputation to uphold.

Crop rotation. If you grow the same crop on the same ground year after year the soil will deteriorate and the quality of the crop decline. A careful plan of cropping over a three or four year period will prevent this happening and will also utilise the ability of one crop to help the one that follows. In this way a crop like potatoes follows a crop such as cabbage, which needs plenty of manure. The following rotation plan works well and involves dividing the plot up into three areas. If you like, keep to this overall plan, reducing its scope to your particular requirements.

	Plot A	*Plot B*	*Plot C*
Year 1	Cabbage	Peas	Carrots
	Brussels Sprouts	Beans	Beetroot
	Broccoli	Celery	Swede
	Cauliflower	Leeks	Parsnips
		Lettuce	Potato
		Tomatoes	Turnip
		Onions	

Year 2	Carrots Beetroot Swede Parsnips Potato Turnip	Cabbage Brussels Sprouts Broccoli Cauliflower	Peas Beans Celery Leeks Lettuce Tomatoes Onions
Year 3	Peas Beans Celery Leeks Lettuce Tomatoes Onions	Carrots Beetroot Swede Parsnips Potato Turnip	Cabbage Brussels Sprouts Broccoli Cauliflower

Storing the crop

Carrots can be stored in boxes of dry sand in a frost free place. The tops are cut off and the sound carrots laid in rows with either sand or peat laid between each row. *Beet* are stored in the same way but the tops are twisted off; if the leaves are cut off there is a danger of bleeding. *Onions* are stored by being made up into a rope and hung in a frost free place. Another method is to use old stockings, tying a knot in the stocking as each onion is inserted. They must have good air circulation if they are to last. Store *marrows* by laying them on a bed of straw and putting more straw on top. This can only be done satisfactorily in a dry shed and like other storage conditions it must be free of frost. *Parsnips, turnips and swedes* do not need storing as if they are left in the ground they will not come to any harm. *Potatoes* can be stored in sacks or brown paper bags.

No matter what the crop is the storage conditions must be dry and frost free. The vegetable must be clean and undamaged and some air circulation in the store cuts down the possibility of deterioration.

Fruit in the small garden

Whatever you choose to grow in the way of fruit your nursery catalogue will advise you in detail about flavour, pollinators, and hardiness of the many excellent varieties now available.

Soil preparation is much the same as for any other plant, with plenty of well rotted manure or compost worked as deeply as possible into the soil. Planting means the digging of a hole large enough to take the roots when they are spread as widely as possible and deep enough to allow the soil to come to the same level as it was in the nursery.

Before planting, examine the roots and cut back any that are damaged or over-long. Make a small heap of top soil in the bottom of the hole for the tree to rest on then position the tree in the centre of the hole. If you have a standard tree that needs staking, drive the stake well into the ground *before* planting.

Once the tree or bush is positioned, the fine soil should be worked into the roots: move the tree gently up and down to get the soil well into the finer roots and then firm well down. Fill the hole, firming well as you go so that the tree cannot move even in the strongest winter wind. If your soil is poor give a top dressing of manure. Do not prune in the first year after planting and then prune hard the following winter (see p. 187).

Varieties of fruit

Apples. Many apple trees are self-sterile which means that they need the pollen from a different variety of apple to make the flowers set and produce fruit. These need another tree planted nearby to act as pollinator. Varieties that do not need this help are called self-fertile and will get on perfectly well in isolation. Even with self-sterile varieties, it does not mean that you *must* buy another tree simply to act as a pollinator: your next door neighbour may well have a tree in his garden that will do the job, and bees don't worry a lot about fences and hedges.

Most nursery catalogues include in their fruit section details about suitable pollinators, so if the variety you choose is not self-fertile, like Lord Lambourne or Epicure, then the selection of a suitable tree needs a little care.

An easy way out of this difficulty is to plant Family Fruit Trees. A tree of this sort is worked onto rootstocks of medium vigour so that they do not grow too large for the smaller garden. On each tree you will find three different varieties of apples which cross-pollinate each other so that on one tree you could have Scarlet

Pimpernel (July August), George Cave (August) and Queen Cox (October January)—three delicious dessert apples for use over a period of time. There are six different assortments of apples so you could have both dessert and cooking apples on the same tree. They should be planted 14 foot apart at least, and if you want to move them this is no problem during the first eight years. Move house and take your orchard with you.

Traditional apple trees come in various forms. Standards have bare stems 6 feet long and half-standards have bare stems 3 to 4 feet tall. Trees of this sort should be planted 25 to 30 feet apart. Bushes should have 18 to 24 feet between them while cordons, which are single stem trees planted in rows with each stem sloping at 45°, need only 2 to 3 feet between trees. Trained and shaped trees like espaliers and fan shapes need 16 to 24 feet between them.

Apples are invariably grafted or budded onto a rootstock and the selected rootstock affects the habit of the tree. For the garden, rather than commercial growing, you are looking for rootstocks that do not give vigorous growth but at the same time encourage early fruiting. MII, MVII, MIX, MM106, MM109 and MM111 are frequently used on small trees while for Standards MXVII is ideal.

In general terms apples should not carry a crop for the first two or three years after planting but if you do not get fruit after four or five years then it may either be because the soil is too rich and the tree is putting on wood instead of fruit, or perhaps because there is no suitable pollinator handy.

Pears. As with apples you must make sure that the tree you plant has a suitable pollinator close by and again there are two different assortments of Family Fruit Trees to provide the dessert fruit that you need. Planting distances and cultural requirements are the same as for apples, but pears do not need such deeply dug soil to give of their best.

Plums. Easy to grow, plums do particularly well in limey soils. They need little or no pruning and several varieties are self-fertile although others do need a pollinator. Self-fertile varieties include Victoria and Czar.

Raspberries. A rich well dug soil is called for, so work plenty of well rotted manure into the soil. Once the canes are established the soil should be disturbed as little as possible as raspberries are surface rooting and digging can harm them. Because of this surface rooting, raspberries will suffer badly if allowed to dry out in hot weather. After planting, cut the canes back to 9 inches and after fruiting cut the old wood back to ground level. Plant 18 inches apart with 4 feet between the rows.

Gooseberries. Gooseberries are not difficult to grow but for the best results you need to add potash to the soil. Make sure the fertiliser that you use is high in potash and if you thin the fruit you will have a fine crop. Plant 4 to 5 feet apart.

Strawberries. Rich, well dug ground plus an annual dressing of balanced fertiliser is the secret of success. Plant 15 inches between plants and 24 inches between the rows. The bed you lay initially will last for three or perhaps four years when a new bed must be laid down. Use runners from the parent plant for this, so that the bed is self-perpetuating.

28

Winter protection of tender plants

GORDON COOPER

Here to end with is a little problem that bothers some people. Many of the plants in the garden survive the winter perfectly well; others go dormant, many of them losing all their top foliage like perennial plants. Annual, seed raised plants have finished their growth cycle, leaving seed to be sown next spring. There are, however, a number of varieties that will get through the cold spell only if they are given some protection. For small plants this can be done by lifting them and storing them in frost free conditions, but for other larger plants this is not practical and the protection must be provided *in situ.*

Dahlias. Once the foliage has been blackened by the first frost, it is cut away down to 6 inches above ground level and put on the compost heap. The tubers are carefully lifted, washed and dried before being stored in sand or dry peat in a box kept in a frost free place. Remember to label them as you lift, and give each tuber a dusting with Flowers of Sulphur as a precaution against mildew. As the stems are hollow it is worth storing them upside down to allow any moisture to drain away. Do not store Dahlia tubers in a dry hot cupboard, as this dries them out. A dry frost free spot is all you need.

Tuberous Begonias and Gloxinias. Lift them in October and store the tubers in dry peat until the spring, when they are started into growth again.

Geraniums. More correctly called pelargoniums, these plants can make fine pot plants for winter colour as well as being used for bedding purposes. They are wintered by taking cuttings in late summer and kept in a cool greenhouse to make new plants that will flower the following year. If you do not have a greenhouse then the cuttings can be kept indoors. Some people do not take cuttings, but simply box up the old plants and keep them in a dry shed. If the winter is not severe these can succeed.

Fuchsias. Fuchsias, like many other greenhouse plants, can also be used in the open garden but in this case they must be brought in for the winter and potted up. Reduce the amount of water they receive gradually, until the soil is only just above bone dry, and start them off again in the spring by increasing the water. Hardy fuchsias like F. Riccartonii are quite happy in the open garden for the winter.

Protection for outdoor plants. Many of the plants put into the garden in the autumn will need some protection if they are to get through their first winter. Conifers in particular are frequently damaged by cold winds and a screen of hessian or polythene supported on strong stakes will provide the protection they need. For more tender plants put four stakes around the plant and secure hessian all round. The space in the centre can be filled with straw for extra protection. Climbing plants are protected in much the same way but, in this case, the stakes are leaned against the wall and the hessian laid across them, forming a lean-to shelter. This can also be filled with straw for extremely tender subjects.

Index

Compiled by Gordon Robinson